Positive

SPORTS

Professional athletes

and mentoring youth

by

Debbie
Elicksen

Freelance Communications
Calgary, Alberta
www.freelancepublishing.net

National Library of Canada Cataloguing in Publication

Elicksen, Debbie
Positive Sports: Professional athletes and mentoring youth
by Debbie Elicksen. 1st - edition.

Includes bibliographical references.
ISBN 0-9730237-3-2

1. Athletes—Biography. 2. Mentoring. I. Title.
GV697.A1E44 2003   796'.092'2   C2003-911219-5

© 2003 Debbie Elicksen
ISBN 0-9730237-3-2

Publisher:
Freelance Communications
Calgary, Alberta
Canada
Phone: (403) 240-1340
Fax: (403) 249-4249
Email: freelancecommunications@shaw.ca
Website: www.freelancepublishing.net

Printed and bound in Canada
Copyright 2003

Cover design and layout: Nadien Cole Advertising
Photographs:
       Front Cover—Debbie Elicksen, Getty Images
       Back Cover—Peter Maher
       Inside: Debbie Elicksen, Signature Entertainment,
       Mette Juliussen
Printer: Friesens Book Division, Altona, MB

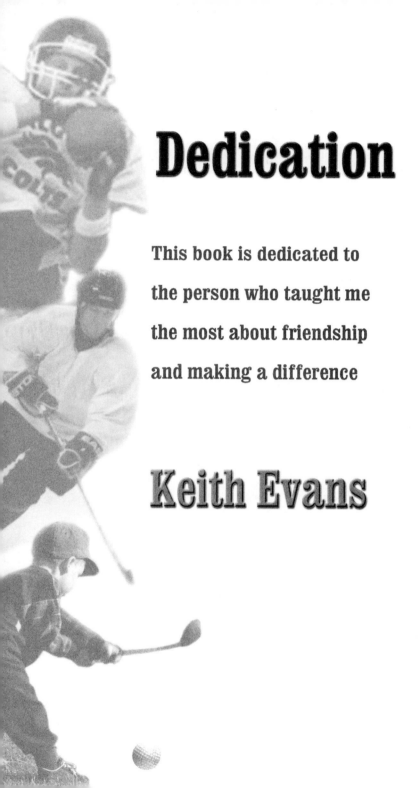

Dedication

This book is dedicated to
the person who taught me
the most about friendship
and making a difference

Keith Evans

Acknowledgements

The following people were instrumental in providing me with the text for this book by their generous offering of time: Jarome Iginla, Paul Kariya, Dan Bylsma, Mark McLoughlin, Stephane Yelle, Jamie Storr, Ian Laperriere, Doug Gilmour, Joe Juneau, Garry Sawatzky, Mike Egener, Corey McNabb, April Clay, Jayson Krause, Willie O'Ree, and Helen Wong (National Basketball Association).

It's impossible to embark on such an undertaking without the support from colleagues and friends...in particular, Ron Fujikawa. I can't say enough about the help and guidance he's provided me over the years. Without him, I'm quite sure this book would not have been written. I also appreciate the kind words, friendship and support of Chris and Richard Saint Marche, Keith Evans, Stan Schwartz, Doug Rooke, Donna Matheson, Mette and Austen Juliussen, Audrey Bakewell, Deb Matejicka, Lisa Hillary, Sheri Hargrave, Rich Lamarche, Art Breeze, Brent Breeze, Kathy Van Heurn, Peter Hanlon, Sean O'Brien, Bernie Hargrave, Harold Grace, Don and Molly Henderson, Arnie Jackson, Billy Powers, and the person who most influenced my life direction, Stan Fischler.

Table of Contents

Foreword **8**

Introduction **9**
How sports and athletic role models provide positive influences   9
Societal and modeling impact on youth identity   11
Sport as a nurturing environment   13
Role model importance   15

Chapter One – The Impact of Sport **16**
Benefits to youth—what do they get out of it?   16
Examples – stories of individuals inspired by sport   18
   • Mike Egener, Western Hockey League player   18
   • Jayson Krause, Canadian National Bobsleigh Team   23
   • Garry Sawatzky, Canadian Football League player   30

Chapter Two – Challenges at the Grassroots Level . . **37**
Funding cutbacks to sport programs   37
Negative impacts   40
   • Winning at all costs   40
   • Abusive coaches and parents   41
   • Bad press for high profile athletes   43

Chapter Three – Programs **46**
Basketball Without Borders   46
National Basketball Association Read to Achieve   47
National Hockey League Diversity Program   48
Hockey It Pays   52
Hockey Canada Initiation Program   54
Youth Football Clinics   64
Baseball Tomorrow Fund   65
Reviving Baseball in Inner Cities   66

Chapter Four – Role Models 67

Shareef Abdur-Rahim, National Basketball Association Forward   67
Ray Allen, National Basketball Association Guard   68
Shawn Bradley, National Basketball Association Center   69
Dan Bylsma, National Hockey League Right Wing   70
Vince Carter, National Basketball Association Guard   73
Tyson Chandler, National Basketball Association Forward   75
Michael Curry, National Basketball Association Forward   76
Dale Davis, National Basketball Association Center/Forward   77
Vlade Divac, National Basketball Association Center   77
Tim Duncan, National Basketball Association Forward/Center   78
Adonal Foyle, National Basketball Association Forward   79
Lawrence Funderburke, National Basketball Association Forward   80
Doug Gilmour, National Hockey League Center/Left Wing   81
Brian Grant, National Basketball Association Center   84
Allan Houston, National Basketball Association Guard   86
Juwan Howard, National Basketball Association Forward   87
Larry Hughes, National Basketball Association Guard   88
Jarome Iginla, National Hockey League Right Wing   89
Antawn Jamison, National Basketball Association Forward   92
Joe Juneau, National Hockey League Center   93
Paul Kariya, National Hockey League Left Wing   95
Jason Kidd, National Basketball Association Guard   97
Ian Laperriere, National Hockey League Center   98
George Lynch, National Basketball Association Forward   100
Karl Malone, National Basketball Association Forward   100
Shawn Marion, National Basketball Association Forward   101
Donyell Marshall, National Basketball Association Forward   102
Tracy McGrady, National Basketball Association Guard   103
Mark McLoughlin, Canadian Football League Kicker   104
Gary Payton, National Basketball Association Guard   112
Jalen Rose, National Basketball Association Guard/Forward   113
Bryon Russell, National Basketball Association Forward   114
Brian Shaw, National Basketball Association Guard   115
Eric Snow, National Basketball Association Guard   116

Jerry Stackhouse, National Basketball Association Forward   117
Jamie Storr, National Hockey League Goaltender   118
Damon Stoudamire, National Basketball Association Guard   122
Kurt Thomas, National Basketball Association Forward/Center   123
Antoine Walker, National Basketball Association Forward   123
Chris Webber, National Basketball Association Forward   124
Corliss Williamson, National Basketball Association Forward   125
Stephane Yelle, National Hockey League Center   126

Conclusion 129

Bibliography 131

Interviews 136

Websites 136

About the Author 137

Reader Survey 138

Foreword

Hi, my name is Austen. I am nine years old and I really, really like golfing. I like golfing because I feel like I'm just like Tiger Woods.

I like Tiger Woods because I think he is the best golfer in the world. He's always nice to kids and other people. He's really cool and seems like a really nice person.

I started golfing when I started to walk. I go with my Grandpa. We golf together and I even have my own set of clubs. I shoot right and Grandpa shoots right. We go to the driving range too. I take golfing lessons too.

What I also like best about golfing is I get to spend time with my Grandpa. Last year, I beat my Grandma in a golf game. She gave up in the middle of the game.

I hope I can become just like Tiger Woods and play with the pros.

Austen Juliussen

Introduction

How sports and athletic role models provide positive influences

April Clay is a Chartered Psychologist whose independent practice focuses on the areas of counseling, consulting, equine assisted psychotherapy, and sport psychology. In the case of role models, she observes that adults will make judgments based on a person's exterior, while kids see something different.

"A kid is more likely to be taking in the experience of the person rather than appearance. We've (adults) built up more negative associations with certain things. Fortunately, kids are much more open to people. They go by how they feel around the person and the experience.

"I work with horse riders a lot and it's quite a unique experience. It's the only sport where children have to deal with a teammate that isn't human and doesn't speak English. That leads to all sorts of interesting dynamics. In the horse industry, the attitude toward the horse has evolved. It used to be that the horse was a tool. The horse had to serve you. Its feelings weren't really regarded and its world wasn't taken into account. It was something you used to get to your goal. Now with the shifting in the horse industry, people are coming forward and saying, we need to understand the horse is an animal and it has a different experience than we do. We have to work with that rather than just dominating it. We have to try to understand its language...form a communication. From tool to partner. I just find that interesting in what it's encouraging children to do. It's much more healthy in terms of role model with a horse because they are being encouraged to respect the horse, to understand its language, and partner with them instead of controlling them. That kind of learning opportunity can be transferred. Horses now are being used therapeutically to help

challenged youth in a non-riding environment. Just being around them and working with them, solving problems because of its reason. The other thing about horses is they give you such honest feedback on how you're treating them. If you've got an angry kid who is used to getting his needs met at home by being angry and by being forceful, and tries to work that with a horse, the immediate feedback is that it's not going to work. They're going to have to develop different skills that they might not get at home because they may be conditioned to being forceful. A horse isn't going to tolerate that. If they love the horse, they might start to develop skills, like stepping back and trying something different. The horse can actually be a role model. Their only fundamental will is to survive. They don't have any hidden agenda. They don't have any stuff about winning. They want to survive. You can use force, but in the end, it wouldn't really work in a team situation any more than it would work with a horse. It might work for a short period of time, then it will break down."

Clay also recognizes how important it is for kids to see themselves in their role models. *"I think minorities would say it's difficult when you never see an image of yourself anywhere on television or in advertisement. The same thing goes with sport - it's another mirror or opportunity to write an invitation. It would be important to try to encourage diversity at grass roots level and give the opportunity to children from different cultures to try sports that they might not have otherwise have tried. In terms of giving kids more exposure to people of different cultures - when you think about the movie "Remember the Titans" (Walt Disney Pictures, Jerry Bruckheimer Production), it's a good example of how (the teammates) started out with all of these prejudices and preconceived assumptions of one another. Because they were forced to work together, they had to start breaking those down. It was a really nice example of what happens in the end - you have this new group identity. For instance, a gay player, outside of the team, might not be accepted or befriended, but because he's in that team situation, people have to challenge their own assumptions about gay people."*

When kids don't see a mirror image of themselves in the media, Clay explains, *"It makes it more difficult for a person to even see the possibility or have the belief because you don't see an example of it. You have to create that. It gives those people double the challenge that others have because you're still dealing with the challenges of getting there. On the other hand, having a ready example to look at says, because I'm like that person, I look like that person, I come from the same culture, I can do that."*

Societal and modeling impact on youth identity

Internal struggles are greatly impacted by the outside world and how a child is perceived or how he or she perceives themselves amongst his peers. Kids turn to their peers for validation. Abraham Maslow describes that every individual's esteem is motivated by the need to belong. An identity crisis occurs when the child has difficulty in finding his or her own niche or someone to believe in. As they rebel against their parents' values, they turn to an external source for identification, even if it's a musician, movie star, or athlete. It's not uncommon to see kids identify with rebellious singers like Eminem or Marilyn Manson or want to imitate heroes like Wayne Gretzky, Nicolas Cage, or Tiger Woods.

The social learning theory (Bandura, Ross, and Ross) portrays that children learn patterns of behavior from informal observation of live and filmed models. The child sees a model displaying aggressive behavior as having given them permission to exhibit similar behavior. It's more likely a child will show aggressive behavior when a real-life model is aggressive, but film, television, musician, and athletic models are also just as influential.

When parents are increasingly absent, peers, television, and day cares take on the role of parent. Clinical and Developmental Psychologist, Dr. Gordon Neufeld, says peer-orientation is evident in every playground and school. The attempt to win approval from peers strengthens mob mentality. If the worst behaved kids spend most of their time with other kids, they have difficulty in maintaining their own identities.

Regardless of economic background, kids who experience parental apathy or disapproval are more apt to become influenced by external sources. As recreational and social programs are chopped due to financial constraints, kids turn to gangs or other sources for the sense of family they're not getting at home. An abundance of free time can lead to adverse behavior in order to combat boredom.

Positive growth and identity is developed through activities that are constructive, enhance feelings of self worth, and which provide positive models of behavior. For instance, school mentorship programs, tutoring, computer literacy programs, sports, recreation, and arts programs all contribute to a child's self-esteem. They help combat stress and can ultimately prevent gang membership.

What kind of stress does today's youth face? In 1993, the Canadian Psychiatric Association surveyed 800 teens across Canada, aged 13 to 18, on the biggest sources of teen stress. The results showed that over half of Canadian youth are highly stressed and have a general sense of hopelessness. Fifty-one percent felt stressed as often as once a month to few times a week, while one in three experienced depression at same frequency. Twenty-three percent encountered times when they thought they might have serious emotional problems. Nineteen percent thought about suicide, and of those, twenty-two percent had made an attempt. The survey also revealed that teens attribute their stress to:

School – 65 percent (grades, teachers, homework, violence)
Home/Family – 11 percent
Friends/Relationships – eight percent
Finances/Money/Work – four percent
Other (future, health, drugs) – nine percent

Sports as a nurturing environment

In adolescence, the desire for self-importance is so strong that it becomes a primary need. A study by John C. Coleman tabulated the impact of peer group values from ten schools. The students were asked how they best wanted to be remembered. Boys preferred to be known as the best athlete nearly twice as often as being known as the best student. The study also concluded that in order to become part of the leading crowd, boys would be judged on their sporting ability, personality, and good looks.

Albert Bandura reveals that chance encounters are also important to youth. Some will touch kids lightly while others will influence them greatly. After a professional sports event, some of the visiting stars might find a shortcut to exit the building and avoid any fans that may be waiting for them in the concourse. They may do this for a couple of reasons, one being that if they stopped to write an autograph for every person, the team would never make its chartered flight. Another reason may be that they cannot be bothered to sign autographs or that if they sign a few and miss some, those missed will have an adverse perception of that player.

Many times, life experiences are determined by chance. When an adolescent's values are identified, he or she will lean towards activities and people that reflect those values. However, powerful group influences can still undermine the best-laid personal affirmations. Groups offer a symbolic environment and an opportunity to build self-knowledge and shape identity. The group can strengthen beliefs and provide self-efficacy.

Society in particular, splits boys into two selves by discouraging them from showing public affection or sensitivity while insisting they be tough and reticent. This conflicts with their inner feelings and adds to their frustration when they are viewed upon as being insensitive, uncaring, and violent. In his book, "Real Boys" (Henry Holt and Company, New York ISBN 0805061835), William Pollack writes that boys feel like they can open up in a sporting environment. They can be more comfortable about nurturing and caring for each other in the context of the playing field. Passion, emotions, love, and affection are all acceptable feelings and shame-free. Sport teaches boys to how to handle adversity and loss, how to be flexible, and how to excel at something that comes naturally. Sport offers boys a community of support that can ultimately lead to life-long friendships.

In sport, the coach largely creates the emotional environment. It is an integral part of the development of a child's self-esteem and their connection with the group. A coach can help transform a young person's feeling of isolation into that of a bonded teammate. As a stand-in for a parent, the coach determines whether the child's experience on the team is positive or negative. A bad coach will use humiliation and bullying tactics to push the athlete to work beyond his or her natural skill level, thus producing feelings of resentment, shame, and indifference. One of the ways these types of coaches motivate players to improve their game is by inflating the capabilities of their opponents and downgrading those of their own team.

Self-efficacy is as important as skills are to success in sports. If a player believes in his or herself, their ability to capitalize on their own physical strength and endurance will increase during competition. Even if the athlete fails to make a play or loses the game, their perceived self-efficacy will push them to greater efforts in the next play or the next game. A person's belief system is the key to how they view the extent to which their environment can be influenced and controlled. In other words, you act as you think.

Perceived self-efficacy can also be a motivator. If the athlete's self-efficacy is high, even mistakes or pressure situations will push them to succeed. They'll take the game one play at a time. On the other hand, if a player is filled with self-doubts, they will struggle through and exasperate their mistakes. They'll be more inclined to settle for mediocrity. Self-efficacy can also affect how a player bounces back from injury. If their perceived self-efficacy is lacking, they may dwell on his or her physical discomfort and let it distract their performance.

Role model importance

Everyone is motivated by the need to belong, to be loved, and to build esteem. Peers and models can sometimes be the only influence available to help create a strong self-efficacy. It's a role many professional athletes do not take lightly.

In the book, *"Inside the NHL Dream"* (Freelance Communications, ISBN 0973023708), National Hockey League star Paul Kariya, discusses the importance of being a good role model. *"It's really important for us. When I was growing up, Wayne Gretzky was my role model. I'd like to think he had a lot of impact on the way I handle myself on and off the ice. If I can help one kid out by leading a good example and playing hard every night, and off the ice, staying out of trouble, it's good."*

Debbie Elicksen

Chapter 1

The Impact of Sport

Benefits to Youth - what do they get out of it?

It's the yearning for connection. When teammates congratulate a receiver and tell him how proud they are for his making the big catch, it's pure intimacy. Sports offer a community of support - something that is quickly disappearing from our individual neighborhoods.

Who do kids look up to? Who are their real heroes? The Search Institute (a non-profit organization that provides practical research, which benefits children and youth) says during the first 18 years of life, it is common for young people to be strangers in their own neighborhood. Their research shows that fewer than one in five kids believed that their neighbors cared about them and they didn't know many adults outside of their own family very well.

With parental presence diminishing - children are being raised, more or less, by their peers and the mass media. They spend too much time alone at home. On top of that, too many adults fail to model or even value caring behavior. It's the very reason why it's essential for adults to respond because they are the ones who have often failed in their responsibility.

Through its research, the Search Institute has discovered that positive outcomes in a kids' behavior increases with each additional number of available adults. Spontaneous and sustained relationships with adults outside of the home are at the center of a healthy community for youth.

Our culture tends to focus on young people's problems and there is a hopelessness and powerlessness among adults in finding the solution. Few believe they have the capacity to intervene and would rather avoid young people than get involved.

During the 1996 United States presidential campaign, First Lady, Hillary Clinton, repeated the African wisdom that "it takes a whole village to raise a child". Unfortunately, society's focus on services has affected our sense of community. If everyone reclaimed or accepted their shared responsibility to nurture the youngest generation, kids would have a better shot at being groomed into becoming caring adults and turning to positive activities.

Adults tend to use perceived lack of time or their being uncomfortable with youth as an excuse not to get involved. The Search Institute has discovered that mentoring programs can reduce the onset of alcohol and other drug use, inhibit personal violence, and improve school attendance.

"Sports can take on the role of being a second family," says April Clay, Chartered Psychologist and member of the Sport Psychology Association of Alberta. *"Kids see these people on a regular basis and can form a really close relationship. The group may provide a sense of stability that isn't happening at home. The child may not have consistent parenting or caring parents. In the sport environment, there may be some adults - coaches and parents, who provide them with a different kind of experience, of consistency and security. In a difficult home environment, lack of consistency and conflicting messages can really damage. There may also be physical abuse. Sport gives kids another environment that lets them get to know themselves differently.*

"There are lots of benefits to sports besides promoting exercise and movement...mastering physical skills. In terms of the psychological side, kids have access to people and role models that they might not otherwise be exposed to. That can be good and bad. There are more examples for them to learn from. Learning a set of responsibilities, meeting a goal, setting goals, learning how to

interact in a team situation, develop social skills, understanding self discipline, and delayed gratification - having to sacrifice something to get something you want. Patience, setting up a goal, and working towards something."

Examples – stories inspired by sport

Mike Egener

Picked by Tampa Bay (from Florida) in the second round of the 2003 NHL Entry Draft, 34th overall, this young defenseman is known as much for his off-ice contributions as he is for his on-ice skills. In fact, 18-year-old Mike Egener received the ENMAX Humanitarian Award in 2002 for his dedication to the Calgary community.

Egener credits much of his character to his family's support. *"There are a lot of things important in life but most important is your family...especially mine. They're always there to back me up. I'm so fortunate to have two parents and siblings, who I'm best friends with. Both my parents have always done the best they could. I remember my dad making us a backyard rink. We'd be out there until 10:00 on school nights. It would be minus whatever outside and we'd still be playing. My mom has always been there to help me with my school, always cooking us the most amazing dinners. My sisters have always been there to support me, my brother too."*

Mike Egener

His appreciation for his family is especially strong when he thinks about the recent war in Iraq. *"You really see how*

18

fortunate you are to have family. Especially since in third world countries, not necessarily Iraq, they don't always have a house to live in. I've always had everything I need. All that goes to my parents."

There were several positive adult influences outside the home too. *"Not so much my coaches, but one in particular, believed in me. Mr. Thompson was my coach in Barrie, Ontario. I remember one teacher I had in Kingston in grade four. She taught me how to properly handshake, and when you meet someone, to look them in the eye. I've always remembered that. It's interesting that I can remember that from grade four.*

"Another teacher in grade nine, when I was living in Barrie, Mr. Faye - he was someone that really inspired me. He was always happy and he cared for every student. It didn't matter if he or she was a bad student or a good student, he treated them exactly the same. We stayed in touch when I moved out west and he sent me a piece of paper I had written on. It asked what I wanted to be and I said, a bouncer at the Rock, which was a bar. After that there was a slash, then it said, an NHL hockey player. On the back, it had my signature and number 4, the number I wear now but it wasn't my number then. I gave him a four-leaf clover. He traveled a lot and went around the world with that in his wallet. That meant a lot to me. I didn't think he'd actually care about that stuff...a grade nine student giving that to him.

Playing in the same rink as the Calgary Flames, Egener is afforded an access to NHL players that most other kids are not. *"Everyday, we get to see the Flames practice, in addition to the different teams that come into town. None of the players are too cocky or too good for you. One in particular, Gary Roberts, who used to play in Calgary, was always a genuine nice guy. He'd walk by one of the guys and say, "Hey buddy." It's just hearing that from an NHL player. We look up to them so much. It's like younger kids looking up at us. I remember when I was younger and getting his hockey stick. That meant so much - for these guys to sign something. For the rest of the day, I'd be the happiest kid. Now it's a chance for us to do that with someone else - the younger kids. It doesn't take very much time to do that. It means a lot to us because we're giving back.*

"Growing up, we moved around quite a bit because my dad was in the army. I lived in Barrie, Ontario, where the Colts Ontario Hockey League team plays; in Fredericton, New Brunswick - that team isn't there anymore. We used to watch the Kingston Frontenacs. The players that made the most influence on me were probably the Fredericton Canadiens. A lot of them are now playing in Montreal in the NHL because it was their farm club. I remember watching the Toronto Maple Leafs training camp in Barrie. Doug Gilmour was my favorite player at the time. When he came off the ice, there were a bunch of kids asking for autographs. He chose me and another kid. For us, it was very special."

Egener knows a player can't always sign every autograph due to charters and timelines. *"If he didn't choose your autograph, you would have probably been disappointed. When you get on the bus, as a player, you do wish you could have signed more autographs. Unfortunately, some people might think the players are too hot headed - that they don't want to sign. A lot of people don't realize the stuff that's going on. They don't always have that time. There are things players have to do with the team."*

On community service: *"Every month there are about three of us who go to the Children's Hospital to visit the kids. Each player has a police officer that we get to go on ride-alongs with. My officer really wanted to see the kids because he actually had cancer before and could relate to them. He and I would go visit the kids every month.*

"I've really gotten to know one kid in particular. His name is Michael. He really struck me. You go in there and see a lot of

positive kids. They surprise you how cute they are and how unfortunate it is they are in the hospital. They're so young. They shouldn't be there. When I first came to see Michael, he had an intriguing imagination. He was very smart. He's always happy. He really inspired me and the other guys that went with me. I couldn't believe the questions he was asking about hockey. It was unfortunate for a kid like him to be there. He's only about 12 or 13. For the situation he's in, he does an amazing job of it.

"Going to the hospital - before I wouldn't have the chance to do that. Hockey has given me an opportunity to do this. It's something that's really helped me out - making me realize how fortunate I am to not be in their situation. You see them fighting their injuries and it just makes you stronger and want to try your best to put a smile on their face.

"For our Sunday afternoon games, I've got a thing with a tanning salon for kids who can't afford tickets. They come down after a game and I bring over a couple of teammates so they can ask questions and get autographs. Anytime our Public Relations Director, Charla Odgers, ever needs anything, I try my best to make time available."

While inspired by some of his NHL heroes, Egener realizes fan perception of professional athletes can be negative. *"It's just like anything you're not involved with. For example, regarding the war in Iraq, I don't know enough about it to make a distinct view on it. I can't really say, I don't think they should be going to war or they should be. I just don't know too much about it. I shouldn't be getting into it if I don't know anything. That's just the same with hockey. A lot of people can say their views but they don't actually know what's happening in the dressing room. We've got a pact - what happens in the dressing room, stays there. People see what's going on the ice but they don't really know. I haven't been playing that long but I see the fan's perspective. I see the hockey. But when you're on the bench, you see the slashes. You hear the dirty talking*

- all that kind of stuff. They'll say their view but they don't know what a player is all about. Everyone has a different personality. You're going to find a diamond in the rough - those guys that are going to help out outside of hockey. Every team is going to have a few of those.

"People have to realize that hockey players have lives too. If you make a mistake, so what? You don't need to jump on someone's back for that kind of stuff. Every day people are going to make mistakes. You see it in every day life in the newspapers. Usually what the reporters jump on people's backs for are just minor things that don't really matter much, but they escalate them into bigger things. Fortunately, for myself, I haven't had one of those instances and hopefully I won't. I generally get along with the reporters pretty well. You also have to realize it's their job.

"If I hadn't been involved in sports…I'd still be an interesting person. That's what I think. I'm pretty unique. I'd definitely be going to school. I'm doing that now but I'd be really devoted to it. I'd probably be in university. It's just so fortunate that I stayed with my hockey. When I was younger, I got cut from a team. I thought about quitting. But again, your family is there to support you.

"There are things in life you have to realize. If you don't make it one way, there are always other opportunities. I've got an option where I can play in the NHL if I'm good enough, an option I can play in Europe. In Calgary, I can get five years worth of university because every year is paid for. I'm really glad I'm on this road of hockey journey. I honestly don't know what I'd be doing otherwise.

"I started playing in the Western Hockey League at 16. I'm lucky enough to live at home in Calgary. People don't see how hard it is for kids going away from home at such a young age. A really good friend of mine was living with me. I felt it was really hard for him being away from his home so much. It would be good for any 16

year old to have his parents guide him along. I know it's good for people to learn things by themselves. It's almost like, at 16 years old, you have to be a 20-year-old. That's how quick I had to grow up. I had to learn things about myself, which it's good for you to learn and learn from your mistakes. But it's good to have your parents there to keep you on the right track. I've been so fortunate to have the opportunity to showcase my skills, meet a bunch of great guys, and meet younger kids in unfortunate situations. It's really helped me with my life perspectives. I see things a lot better. The biggest thing I've learned out of all of this is, everyday you've got to work hard. That's all I've done in my whole hockey career. I've just kept with it and worked hard. It's gotten me where I am now and hopefully will get me farther. Anything you do in life, you work hard at it, and you're going to get success."

Jayson Krause

Since entering the bobsleigh scene in 1996, Jayson Krause went from brakeman to piloting his own two-man and four-man team. He and brakeman, Florian Linder, are the youngest full time crew on the World Cup Tour.

"I was playing football and had trouble with injuries. I was really working hard in the off-season on weights and conditioning, but for some reason, I wasn't putting it together during the season. I heard that (Canadian Football League player) Don Blair had average physical skills before his breakout season. The catalyst to his breakout season was that he spent a year bobsledding. It helped his power and speed. I figured, hey, if it worked for him, I'll give it a shot. I went and tried bobsleigh with another teammate, Sherwin Ellis. I didn't post phenomenal numbers, by any means in testing, but my strength was okay. Dave MacEachern talked to me and saw potential in me. He said he won a gold medal as a brakeman in 1998 and he was starting to drive. He needed a young crew to push for him and he was going to fight for a medal in Salt Lake City.

I thought, wow. From playing football with the Colts and now here's an Olympic gold medallist asking me to push for him and travel around the world. It's something I never had intentions of doing. I was just going to use the training as a tool.

"I started training with Dave. During my first season, we went to Europe and competed. It just took off from there. It's amazing how you fall into things by accident.

"When I was a brakeman, it's an explosive start. We hit the sled and try to accelerate it as quickly as possible, then jump in, and go for the ride. We're the horsepower to get the sled moving. For me, because of my size, I was only limited to four-man because I didn't have the mass and height as most bobsledders. I didn't like that. When we were in Europe for six weeks, I was only active, maybe, two or three days a week. It just makes the trip so long when you're sitting around for the other days.

"Then a combination of two things happened - Dave crashing and being forced into retirement and me just wanting to do more. I started driving. Driving is just the complete - it's everything.

"It's so different when I'm standing outside the track and watching sleds go down. It looks fast and crazy but when you're inside the sled, it's like the ultimate focus. It doesn't feel fast. You're dancing with the track. When things are going right and you're driving well, the feeling is incredible. You're so focused and you're coming down the track - everything just fits. It's like the perfect dance. There are a lot of runs where you bang your way down and you're pulling your hair out. Those runs where you experience that perfect dance - it's like hitting the sweet spot on a baseball or a golf club. That's what keeps you coming back.

"There's a lot of training. For what we're training for, it's only used for a maximum five-second push. In the summer, when we train two-a-days, sometimes it's five to six hours. The acceleration

and the power you have to generate are so crucial. There are all the factors that decide how you perform but the push is number one. If you don't have a push, it's very difficult to compete. In football, the training was hard but in a different way. In bobsleigh, everything is so explosive. All the training is jerky with heavy weights and low reps. It's really hard on the joints - all the pounding we do to accentuate the power explosive. Whereas in football you just threw your body in the games and practice. Here it's the training that really destroys the body the most.

"(As a mentor and influence) Dave was incredible. Looking back now and seeing the guys that come and go through the program, the numbers I posted at that time were nothing special. For Dave to take a small guy like me in a sport of giants, believe in me, help me out with money, suiting me up with all the gear I needed... that's incredible that he saw that in me. There are not a whole lot of people who would do that. It's tough to get involved in the sport because of the cost. A lot of people are turned away. I was lucky enough to have the opportunity for Dave to take care of a lot of things for me and believe in me. Through training, I got a lot better quick and then it paid off. Still to this day, him believing in me...

"For the new guys coming in, I do what I can. As a pilot, I'm in control of my own team. I have to recruit and entice people to push for me. I do what I can to help them out. It's not a sport where you get rich but when I make money through my fundraising, I allocate a certain portion of that money to help some of the guys out. Your first year on the national team, you don't get carded. You have no income, even though you start training with the team in September, October, you don't get any income

Jayson Krause

25

*until April. That's a huge sacrifice. I have a little bit of money set
aside where, if guys make the team, I'll give them a bit of money to
help them pay some bills and just make it until they can get their
first carding check from the government. You can't work. You have
to train. You're in Europe. It's extremely hard.*

*"When you're starting off as a crewman, the basic equipment you
need - you have to buy. A helmet is about $400. If you have to buy
bobsleigh start shoes, $300. That's just to be a crewman. Then
there's a jacket and other winter stuff. It gets pretty pricey, aside
from the fact that you have to quit your job. As a pilot, that's when
the real costs get big. Just the blades alone for the bottom of the
sled cost between $8,000 and $10,000 a set. A pilot will have four
to six sets but they generally last the lifetime of your career. That's
$50,000 just in the blades. I bought an old four-man sled for
$25,000. The two-man sled I'm looking to buy is $75,000. I could
stay running with the equipment I have and just try to get by on
improving my push or my driving. But if I really want to fight for a
medal, I have to get the best equipment to complement trying to
achieve the perfect drive or push. The government funding doesn't
help with equipment purchases - it's strictly living expenses. I'm at
the highest level an athlete can get and I get $1,100 a month. As
far as equipment purchases, that's strictly fundraising,
sponsorships, stuff that I have to go out and find people to invest
in my dreams. Everyone has to do it.*

*"Sports, in general, are just an incredible learning tool. When
I was in high school, there was a big debate on destroying
extra-curricular activities that were funded by the government. It's
an ongoing debate. People just don't realize, you can learn from
books and get all this data in your brain, but it's not functional
learning like sports and teamwork. It's so key to learning how to
deal with people, overcoming adversity, teambuilding, and
achieving something. Anyone who has been getting their butt
kicked in a football game in the first half, comes back in the second
half and pulls out that tight win...if you don't experience that,*

you're really missing out. If you don't experience the part of overcoming obstacles in something like sports - there are so many things in sports to teach you lessons. It's underestimated how it can prepare people for future life. You look at the business world...it's the gridiron. It's football. It's a fight to be the best. I think life is like that. I consider myself very lucky. The people I've met...it's like a fraternity. You know people who competed in high performance sports or even high school football, if I run into people that I fought in the trenches with, there's a special bond there that you can never lose.

"There is an adverse side. You can look at it a few ways. As for the coaching aspect, you do run into people that are extremely hard to deal with...We had a coach that was extremely frustrating. There were bits of him that were very good. And as much as I didn't enjoy having him as a coach, in a lot of philosophies, I think he was bang on. He just couldn't execute them properly. I learned as much from him as I have from my current coach, who is absolutely amazing. When you're dealing with different coaches, you have to take the things that you think you can apply. There are things you don't think you can apply, but later on you'll think, he was right. Sometimes you have to take a step back. It's all about learning how to deal with different coaches, just like teammates.

"Regarding the funding aspect, it's tough. It gets really discouraging sometimes. I do so much networking and marketing for myself, when I retire, if I'm applying for a job, I can say, maybe I don't have the degree you're looking for but I've been doing it for six, seven years, and I've been successful at it. As much as it's a drag to have to go and raise funds, at the same time, I'm gaining valuable experience that I can use afterwards.

"I'd definitely like to see bobsleigh be a higher profile sport like it is in Germany or Switzerland. There are a lot of great sports out there that go unnoticed. There's only so much television time and interest for each sport. I think you have to accept that. My best

friend lives with me. He said to me, would you be offended if I told you I wouldn't watch bobsleigh if you weren't in it? If you're not growing up with the hype of bobsleigh, like in some of the European countries, chances are, you're not going to become a hardcore fan. I do it because I like to challenge myself."

On role models: *"There was a guy in the National Football League by the name of Sam Mills. Part of the reason I liked him was because he was a small player in a big man's sport. That was something I dealt with in every sport I went through. Sam Mills was a 5'7" middle linebacker, 200 pounds. He was tough as nails. When you're going against some 300-pound lineman and you're a middle linebacker at 200 pounds, you've got to be tough. Here's a guy who went undrafted out of college. I don't even think he was signed until he had a year out of football, coaching somewhere. Someone in the CFL called him up. He went to the CFL and performed well, went to the NFL, and he ended up making four or five Pro Bowls as one of the best linebackers in the league. That's someone who sort of came out of nowhere, just worked his hardest and pursued his dream of being the best, and there he was, in the Pro Bowl. That's someone I always looked up to. From having to overcome the size deficit...that's incredible.*

"I've been very, very fortunate. Speaking of role models, my dad was an incredible educator. When I speak to groups, I always refer to a lesson my dad taught me when I was a kid. My brother and me were sitting there, when he came and picked us up and said, follow me on your bikes. We biked down this path and stopped in the middle of it. We're thinking, what's going on? He pointed down at this weed growing through the pavement. We thought nothing of it. My dad told us that this weed was growing in the field one day when these workers came across and threw asphalt over top of it. There were a lot of other young weeds that gave up and those weeds died. But this one little weed said, no way, I'm not going to die. I'm going to go get that sunlight so I can survive. This weed fought through every little tiny crack to get to the top. All the

weeds underneath didn't do it except this weed. You saw weeds on the outskirts of the path that were a little green, a little yellow. This weed seems to be the greenest weed around because it fought hard. It went through all the bad stuff it had to, to get to the top.

"At that time, I didn't appreciate it for the lesson it was, but looking back, my dad was a phenomenal educator. There are times when I wanted to give up, where I just wanted to pack it in. I always think of that lesson my dad taught me. That's going to stay with me forever. That's the message I try to convey when I'm speaking to groups. Be like the weed. You've got to fight for what you want. If it's not worth fighting for, it's not worth anything.

"With the initial cost of starting up, I had to sacrifice a lot. Even as a young pilot, I had to buy the blades we run on. I couldn't afford them at first so I had to take a loan from my parents. My parents had supported me a lot. There were a lot of loans I had to take out. I've been able to pay them back but some people don't have the luxury of their parents being able to lend them thousands of dollars. I have a fundraising committee where four of my family members are involved. They work really hard. I have friends, who I compete with on my team, whose families have never seen them compete. My family flew to New York to watch a race at Lake Placid - just to be there to show their support. I'm lucky in so many ways. I used to play the lottery but I stopped playing it because I figured that I'm pretty darned lucky right now. I've won the lottery with all the things that have come my way through family and other things. I'll let someone else have their heyday.

"When I thought of how my life would pan out back before I started bobsledding, I thought maybe I'd be married and have some kids. I'd have liked to be playing football. I remember the year I started bobsledding, University of Manitoba really wanted me to come out there and play football. I was struggling with the idea. I thought no, I really like this bobsleigh thing. I'm going to give it a shot. I still love football but I'm glad I found something that I really, really love."

Garry Sawatzky

Garry Sawatzky was an angry young man growing up in Winnipeg. After one last physical fight with his father, he left home at age 17 and joined a bike gang. He was sentenced to 18 months on a robbery charge and his life took a turn for the worse in 1985, when he was convicted of second-degree manslaughter for stabbing an 18-year-old man to death - a result of a group altercation at a Winnipeg campsite. Garry was 23 when he was incarcerated at Stony Mountain Institution. He got out nine years later at age 32.

His story is a remarkable one because while in prison, the thought of playing football turned his life completely around.

"It was very, very strange because it just came to me. It honestly just came to me. I still don't understand how. I'm an atheist so I don't believe in all that religion stuff. I'm a spiritual atheist. I was in a sweat lodge and it's kind of like, I made a promise. I was in prison. I only had a couple of years in. That's why it was so crazy. Everyone was laughing at me. The bigger I got and the harder I worked towards it, the more it offended people. I wasn't taken very seriously. They said, you're going to be in your thirties when you get out. Nobody's going to touch you. Think! What are you doing? You're pissing me off! And I think that's what happens with kids a lot. They succumb to that crap.

"Right after that, the next thing you know, I'm taking university courses. I found a way to make my own little environment. It was like training camp for the mind and the body. Then I was on a goal. I was on a mission. I completed four training cycles in one year. I had everything planned out. The training cycle went by pretty quick. It made the time go by very fast. Not like, oh, where did the time go? It didn't happen like that. But it did make the time easier."

Inside prison, former Winnipeg Blue Bomber running back, Tim Jesse, saw Garry's physique while visiting the institution. He began to pass the word back to his team and Garry was given an evaluation while on a day pass. The media caught wind of it and the prison then transferred him west to dispel the spotlight. Out of prison, Garry did get the opportunity to tryout for the CFL.

"It was very strange because nothing came instantly. It's like, show up tomorrow and we'll learn how to get into a stance. Show up the next day and we'll learn how to run block. I got out of jail and went to British Columbia Lions after everything blew up in Winnipeg (not getting the shot with the Bombers). I went to B. C. and they brought me back every day. I had three months before camp. I was working two jobs then. I was driving to Surrey every night to learn how to get into a stance. There were no promises at that point. It was pretty unrealistic and a little bit far off. I was just very strong and fast. They figured they could do something with me.

"In my first game, I only played two minutes. I went out for a couple of different series. It was short-lived. I think for the six plays I had, I did okay, but it was like they were just giving me a little taste. That was in 1994, and I was only out of jail for a few months. It freaked me out. I couldn't even get into my football pants. I changed my pants three or four times because I didn't know what size to wear.

They felt so weird every time you put them on. They felt tight but they were baggy. I'd put a tighter one on. I was going out of my mind to find the right pair of pants. I never knew how to wear the stuff since high school."

Prior to prison, he had no role models. *"I was probably lacking in social conscious as well. Kids think they're going to live forever anyway. It's easy to burn candles at both ends. Combine that with early problems in your childhood, and it seems to snowball. When I joined the gang, it was more because there were others like me. We were a new family. I bought into it. Not everyone was into that...not everyone was into the family thing. Everyone was using the club for whatever their gain was - whether it was image or money.*

"My story just isn't about not giving up. I pretty well buried myself and then I had to find a way out. The part about burying yourself, I think a lot of kids learn how to do that. They don't know how to dig themselves back out. I think I found a way to dig myself back out.

"I don't try to understand anything. That's why I don't choose any religions. Everything I do is by feel and not by trying to understand the powerful energy of the universe. Just do what the Indians do, learn to roll with it. They believe in a spirit world and a physical world. You have to show respect because you're a part of it. You can't be more important than a bug. An animal eats a bug, you eat the animal, and so you can't be more important than a bug. I follow that kind of philosophy."

Garry spent the next several seasons playing for more than one CFL team but at the same time, he took the time to reach out to, what society would label as, the unreachable population...kids in prison.

"I think I've been to every kiddie prison in the lower mainland in B. C. I had a friend that was doing some work with the kid prisons out there and he took me to every one. I've even talked to federal inmates. I went back into the joint a couple of times to talk to the lifer group in Stony. I've talked to law students and lots of group homes.

"The kids in prison, I can get right to them. We can cut right through the game. Who's our entertainment today? That's how the kids act. Everything's provided for them. They get into trouble and they get confused. They're still trying to act like those little tough guys and yet down deep, they're still kids. We cut through all that crap. I've been where they are. I know what they're feeling. I know the game. Just cut through the crap. I've got ways of doing it. I've probably learned more from doing that than anything else. When I visit the kids in group homes, they're so unreachable. They're so wound up - so cocky. It's like, when you get in trouble, call me up, and I'll talk to you. There are so many times I've had to talk to them after they've been in jail. It's always after the fact that I have the most success with kids because they're so cocky until they get in trouble. Once everything is taken away, that's the time to rebuild them.

"In talking to kids, I say, daydream about stuff...about things that are mathematically possible. If you make a habit of doing that, if you daydream about things you can actually obtain, you might be far off but it's possible. If it's not mathematically possible, don't dream about it because you're just wasting your energy.

"Football was mathematically possible because I had a plan. Even though I didn't know how I was going to go about it, everything fell into place. It seemed to be luck. You meet the right people. My life is still like that. I'm on the right track. I bump into the right people. They come out of nowhere.

"Join a good gang. Hanging out with the guys, like in football, there are a lot of similarities to the guys in the club. Traveling, having a good time together... joking and getting together to play a game is much more accepted than the guys getting together to go party. You have all these fraternities. Male clubs, where you get together after work. I think it's normal for men to come together as groups. Men feel comfortable in groups...like the hunting and gathering thing. Sports just take the place of that."

While in jail, Garry was enrolled in university courses majoring in philosophy but taking courses in anthropology, sociology, and psychology. He only needs his last five credits to earn his degree. While talking to kids in prison, he came up with another dream, one he is relentlessly pursuing.

"I figure, if you can fix a part of the system and save as many young ones as you can, that's when it really goes around. You can slowly raise the age of a prisoner. The average age of a prisoner is in the early 20s across the board. It should make people freak right out because it's basically, you're kids are in jail. That means for the average age of 21 and 22, there are those that are way too young, which means the guys that are way too old are getting out too easily. Save the young, make room for the old."

His dream is a farm where these types of kids can be isolated from their bad influences and learn to start over - get a new lease on life. *"That would be the long term goal. I want to be careful how I approach this. The system is designed, if you approach anything too aggressively or too quickly to change something, it's going to slap you on the head. You've got to make it so inviting that they want to be a part of what you're making. You have to approach it like, your system is good, and we're just trying to make it better. If you don't approach the system with that attitude, you're going to get slapped.*

"One of the major flaws I see in the system - all of these kids come from different fields. If I go out to any given family, whether it's a nice area or a bad area, I'm finding out people are genuinely the same. They're all on the same level. The same thing is going on in both parts of town. I think people in the nice part of town just hide it. They're not all good homes or support systems. The very first thing they do with a kid coming to jail is to rejoin him with their old support system. Well, the support system he had is what put him there. One of the things you've got to do is wipe out his old support system completely. Take him to a different location than where he lived. If he grew up in B. C., put him in the east coast.

Take him away from the people who made him the way he is. Then only let in the good after that. Have a month chilling out period, where no one can talk to him when he first comes to the facility. Everybody from the outside world has to be cut off until they're deemed good. As soon as they're deemed good, then you can't get enough of them. Show your support.

"It's more of a program. Kids inside can work towards something. It's not just fitting the criteria - you're in, you're not. You can't do it like that. You say, here's a pretty stiff criteria, (and they don't allow this for the system right now because everything has to be for the masses). When you see talent, you've got to capture it. That kid is wasting his time playing with blocks, get him with the other kids that are going to university. The current system has no way of seeing talent or salvaging it.

"Mostly, environment dictates what you're going to be like. You want to create a program to save the ones that are savable. They will present themselves. Here's the step-up-to-the-plate program. Find the kids that are geared for it, just like you do for a business. Business is going to do the proper research to find out their marketing strategies. They go for it and then they win. You've got to do that with the kids. Find out the savable and then save them. I would take a sexually abused kid on my farm but I wouldn't take an abuser. It's not for everyone. There has to be a criteria, and this is going to be my biggest obstacle. The first thing I want to do when I first start getting close to this dream farm is get together an advisory committee. I'd like to sit down all these people I've met - people who would never have been assembled otherwise. They don't all have to have degrees. Get all the good people I've come across, and put them in a room. They have something to give. Put them in a room for a weekend to think and then, take down all the information. Assemble a table of people that are good people, experienced in the field, very intelligent, and futuristic, or have had some success in the past with what I'm doing. I already know where I want to go, but what an ideal way to work out the future headaches."

Does a message from a professional athlete carry more weight?

"It makes a big difference. The kids will give you that instant respect. I've also worked with a lot of coaches. They work hard to get where they are. They worked years with these kids...spent their whole life coaching these kids. And yet, an athlete will pop in for one day and everything is put on him. The coach might think, I'm the guy that helped them get this far and here's this guy for one day. That's the attitude the kids have. They want to be hands on by the real thing. They want real players. It takes a really good coach to be able to share that. I knew this one guy who was so successful as a coach because he didn't have a big ego. Not, no, I don't need any of those guys. There are coaches like that. It's not like the guys don't want to come out and help. I was helping one guy who said to me, any time. He always made me feel like I was appreciated. You don't just want to show up for an appearance. You want them to show up because they're appreciated. I don't mind giving my time. Most of the time they require from athletes is just fluff. Signing stuff. Some players don't do that stuff on their own. Not everyone is giving. Not everyone wants to go and help their fellow man. It's not in everybody."

Chapter 2

Challenges at the Grassroots Level

Funding cutbacks to sports programs

We see it in the headlines every day. Public perception is that amateur sports and recreation always seem to be the first casualties of government funding chopping blocks. It also appears that professional sports teams are never afforded the same axe. Aka government bailout plans for beleaguered owners and lottery licenses being granted to professional sports - all at the expense of the grassroots community.

Marnie McBean is a three-time Olympic gold medallist in rowing. But imagine the fortitude it took to win such a feat, when she had to scrape and scrounge for food and rent. Throughout her training, McBean couldn't afford a car so she biked an hour each direction to and from rowing practice. She later endorsed the Fund for Olympic Rower Survival program in 1996, where $200 would be offered each national team rower (those who were not receiving over $10,000 in sponsorship) each month for seven months of the year.

During its many labor battles, the Calgary Public School Board has raised the issue of chopping high school sports on numerous occasions. Many sports have been cancelled due to teachers' unwillingness to run its programs in the heat of a strike. That means as many as 250 kids could be affected in one school alone. The argument has been that extracurricular activities, such as sports, are not governed by the terms of their employment. Every time a labor battle surfaces, sports ends up becoming the bargaining chip. High school sports programs in other parts of Canada have faced more than a four-year hiatus due to labor strife.

Before Vancouver was awarded the 2010 Winter Olympic Games bid, controversy swirled in the House of Commons when Prime Minister, Jean Chretien, was reported to have bullied the Secretary of State for Amateur Sport, Paul DeVillers, telling him to "sit down and shut up" during a cabinet meeting. Although the intent of the comment was said to be a joke, the incident happened as a result of a lobby to address funding issues for high performance athletes. An extra $10 million bounty was subsequently promised to top Olympic-caliber athletes if Vancouver won the bid for the Games.

What happens when extra-curricular programs are unavailable to youth? Where do they go? Who mentors them? If amateur sport gives an immediate impact to society by teaching young individuals about community, respect, and discipline, what is the alternative when those programs are no longer available?

We may see more violence and weapons in schools, more suicides and substance abuse, more race-related violence, and more kids turning to gangs. While some of the root causes of crime are poverty, racism, poor education, domestic violence, and child abuse, adults lack of attention to youth may be responsible for a cynical generation...one that expects healthcare, education, and social benefits will no longer be available to them when they get older.

Private and public downsizing has contributed to youth unemployment. Statistics Canada reported youth unemployment for July 2003 as 14.1 percent and that 15 to 19 year olds have the least success in finding jobs.

While youth crime in Canada is virtually unchanged from 1998 to 2002, an alarming statistic shows that youth are charged more than twice the rate of adults. In 2002, 4,533 incidents were charged to youth (rate per 100,000 population), while 2,190.9 were charged to adults. Violent crime incidents in 2002, including homicide, attempted murder, and assaults show 933.5 for youth offenders versus 498.1 for adults.

Breaking that down to sexual offences, in 2002, 61% of reported victims were children and youth under age 18. Statistics Canada also shows that 13 and 14-year-old boys are at the highest risk for committing sexual offences.

In the United States, an estimated 2.4 million juveniles were arrested in 2000. Most were held on property charges rather than violent crime. The U.S. Department of Justice reports, between 1995 and 1996, juveniles were more likely to be at risk of being the victim of a violent crime than adults. Those between ages 12 to 14 were more likely to experience simple assault more than older juveniles (73 per 1,000 versus 45 per 1,000).

The need to produce positive environments that help raise youth self-esteem is extremely high. However, corporate philanthropy is mediocre at best. And it takes money to run a sport. Imagine the difference it would make if every business in every community, small or large, donated just one dollar every month to amateur sports? Even one dollar per year. Every business. Every proprietorship, partnership, and corporation. Unfortunately, the sad truth is that only about 10 percent of the business community ever does.

Most community sports programs are non-profit organizations run by volunteer labor. Each year, they struggle to raise funds...usually on efforts that require a high amount of human resources and time for very little return. Corporate sponsorships wane each year but costs for equipment and services keep increasing, putting many programs at risk.

It's a sad testament to our communities when government and corporations would rather put their resources into private enterprise than give an immediate impact to society through amateur sports.

Negative Impacts

Winning at all costs

When he was the head coach of the Vancouver Canucks, Former Vice President of Hockey Canada and Head Coach of the Canadian National Junior Hockey Team, Tom Renney, had parents calling him about the system the Canucks were using on the ice. He responded by telling them to never mind and just go and play.

Winning at all costs is an obsession - particularly in minor hockey. Parents live their dreams of becoming an NHL star through their kids. If their kid becomes the next Paul Kariya, they'll be set for life - financially.

Psychologist, April Clay, adds, "*Winning at all costs, with that kind of value system emphasized, there's that opportunity to take it into their adult life. It's the value of the outcome over people and conducting themselves in a certain way. Being empathetic of others and those types of skills might tend to get underdeveloped because of the overemphasis on outcome. You can see that showing up in a very fundamental level of sports, not just the higher end. If a coach has that kind of a philosophy, whether it's conscious or not, there's a push to buy into that, not just the kids, but also the parents. If they don't, that's where some pretty major conflicts arise. As opposed to those who look at sports as a reason for social involvement, the coach is at the other end of the philosophy. And you can have the opposite. You can have the coach who is trying to emphasize wanting the kids to get some kind of value out of it and the parents saying, I want my kid to win, and why isn't my kid playing today. Then there's everything in between that.*"

Winning at all costs brings on the attitude of teasing and bullying. The coaching staff may even encourage chastising teammates for showing signs of weakness or vulnerability. It gives license to humiliate anyone who contributes to a team loss. It also opens up the possibility of other abuses such as physical and sexual, so that the fear of failure becomes the main motivation. When the fun is taken out of sports, eventually players quit.

Abusive coaches and parents

In 1996, the Western Hockey League was hit with a scandal that rocked the hockey world. Graham James, Part Owner, Head Coach, and General Manager of the Calgary Hitmen, was sentenced to 3 1/2 years for sexually assaulting two former Swift Current Broncos when he coached there from 1986 to 1994. One of those players, Sheldon Kennedy, broke his silence about the assaults he endured while playing for James. He put a human face on the issue. While he had ongoing difficulties sorting through the emotional stress, Kennedy spoke internationally and endorsed a television movie to try and help similar victims get help.

As athletes, players are expected to maintain the overall team image. What happens when a predator unknowingly infiltrates the system as a trusted and respected coach? A young hockey player is at the whim of his coach. In the junior hockey system, the coach decides if you further your career by either playing you, benching you, supporting you, and by pushing you to be better at the game.

When parents live their dreams through their kids and expect them to play like Michael Jordan, April Clay responds, *"There's a child who has already learned there are conditions to his or her worth. It really leads to the development of negative thinking patterns, like perfectionism. Every child's drive is to please the parent. What happens when they grow up is, they take on that thinking style, and there is a very narrow vision of success so they keep driving themselves towards it. If they're not meeting it, then there's something wrong. They're seeing themselves as failures 80 percent of the time. They're not reaching that outcome.*

"I would say (abusive behavior from a coach or parent) comes before that. From what I've seen, there is usually a set of beliefs that would permeate the person's experience or approach to other people. Generally, if the coach is engaged in that kind of behavior, off the field and out of the arena, some aspects of that mirrors at home."

Not all parents are like the New Brunswick dad, who went to court in an attempt to win a Most Valuable Player award he believed was denied his son. But some of the high profile parental abusers seem to take on the form of a tennis coach.

Jennifer Capriati's father, Stefano, was her coach throughout the early part of her career. Due to the enormous pressure he put on her, he pushed her into a high profile burnout. She was fortunate to hire another coach who later helped her revive her career.

Mary Pierce grew up in the shadow of Jennifer Capriati, and like Capriati, her father, Jim (who spent time incarcerated in prisons and mental wards), tried to influence her career. Her father's incessant verbal abuse was landmark. A physical encounter with a bodyguard, at a 1993 tournament in Italy, caused the World Tennis Association to instil the "Jim Pierce Rule" - banning him from attending further matches. At that match, he wielded a knife against the bodyguard Mary hired to protect her and her mother from her father.

The British media dubbed Jelena Dokic's father as the "tennis dad from hell". Damir Dokic started many incidents, throwing tantrums, fighting with tennis officials, chasing camera crews, and even stomping on a reporter's cell phone. He was another father to whom the Jim Pierce Rule was evoked.

Because the International Tennis Foundation recognizes children often have no voice against their parents, it produced a booklet on the subject of burnout. It stemmed from the issue that many parents view tennis and other sports as a road to riches. The ITF booklet warns: *"The success rate at a financially viable level on the professional circuit is minute compared with the dropout rate from lack of talent, injury, or disillusionment."*

Bad press for high profile athletes

Besides Michael Jordan and Shaquille O'Neil, basketball heroes didn't come any bigger than Kobe Bryant. NBA championships under his belt, numerous endorsements, Bryant was considered one of the best-behaved stars in the game. Then something happened on his way to Eagle, Colorado, where he stayed to undergo knee surgery prior to the 2003-2004 season. Bryant was hit with a felony sexual assault charge. Only 24 years old, married with a young baby, Bryant went public to admit he was guilty of adultery but not rape. Speculation swirling, the case is expected to be as big as O. J. Simpson's.

The trial of O. J. Simpson was as big as it got. National football hero charged with two counts of first-degree murder. In 1994, Simpson's ex-wife, Nicole Brown Simpson, and her friend, Ron Goldman, were brutally slain in a driveway. All evidence seemingly pointed back at O.J. From the very beginning, the case monopolized every form of media and was the talk around every water cooler in North America. It began with police chasing a fleeing Simpson in his white Ford Bronco, shown on nearly every television station, to the acquittal after endless months of testimony.

Baseball star, Sammy Sosa, became a household name in 1998 when he and Mark McGuire were locked in a home run battle. McGuire won the title for the year but later admitted taking a performance-enhancing substance, which made Sosa's performance seem pure. In 2003, Sosa made headlines when he used an illegal "corked" bat during a game. All of his records were taken into question while baseball authorities x-rayed every bat in his possession, including those used to obtain those records. Sosa explained, he grabbed the bat by accident, one he only used for batting practice. The rest of his bats were deemed legal and he was given an eight-game suspension, which he was able to reduce to seven on appeal.

In what seemed like a made-for-television movie, National Football League star, Rae Carruth, was sentenced 19 to 24 years for the fatal shooting of his pregnant girlfriend, Cherica Adams. Chancellor, who was seven months in her womb, survived the ordeal. Carruth escaped the death sentence and was charged with conspiring to kill Adams, shooting into an occupied vehicle, and using an instrument to destroy his unborn child. Adams died from a drive-by shooting on November 16, 1999.

Canadian Football League player, Elfrid Payton, who bumped a man with his sport utility vehicle in a restaurant parking lot, punched the same man unconscious after he hit Payton's SUV with his hand. The defensive end was convicted of assault.

Shaquille O'Neil is one of the last NBA stars you would expect to hear anything bad, however, he did receive a one-game suspension and $10,000 fine for slapping Greg Ostertag prior to a season-opening game. O'Neil took responsibility and apologized publicly, owning up to the fact he realized his behavior might affect other people. He asked his young fans not to emulate his conduct.

You don't have to look very far to find negative press on professional athletes. In a lot of cases, the incident may not even warrant a second glance but because the perpetrator was a celebrity, the media knows it sells papers.

Our North American culture is centered around the entertainment industry, to which sports plays a major part. When players cheat and get into trouble, chances are, even if they're incarcerated, there's a good possibility there might be a lucrative book or media contract lurking around the corner.

On the other hand, kids see a double standard. Sports heroes are treated like divine beings at the expense of others.

April Clay: "*I think it would be a confusing experience. If we have a certain perception of a person and something comes along to totally break that apart, we get confused and distressed. If a child has a certain image of a person and all of a sudden an incident draws into question their beliefs, I think it's an important time for parental involvement to help them understand and work through that. It's a good opportunity to talk about things, like people making mistakes and maybe, challenging that kind of putting someone on a pedestal.*"

Chapter 3

Programs

Basketball Without Borders

It's a joint effort between The National Basketball Association (NBA) and the Fédération Internationale de Basketball (FIBA). Basketball Without Borders is a three-day summer camp that was formed in 2001. The program promotes friendship, goodwill, and education through sport. NBA stars serve as coaches. Young participants are selected based on their basketball skills, leadership abilities, and dedication to the sport.

The inaugural Basketball Without Borders was held in Treviso, Italy, in July 2001. Vlade Divac, Toni Kukoc, and five other NBA players from the former Yugoslavia worked with 50 children from Bosnia and Herzegovina, Croatia, FYRO Macedonia, Slovenia, and Serbia Montenegro. In 2002, 50 young Greek and Turkish players in Istanbul, Turkey were led by Hedo Turkoglu and Peja Stojakovic. Basketball Without Borders 2003, held in Treviso, Italy, supported education and HIV/AIDS prevention programs and brought 15 to 17-year-old participants together from across Europe.

"We are very proud to partner again with the NBA for the third edition of Basketball Without Borders after two very successful camps," says FIBA Secretary General, Patrick Baumann. *"The previous camps have proven to be an excellent occasion of young players to get together with their idols. No matter which country they came from, basketball is a universal language."*

Outfitted by sponsors, participants in 2003 were split into four teams without regard to their country of origin. An NBA player was assigned to each team to serve as coach and provide individual instruction. The campers also shared living quarters and sat in on a seminar promoting leadership, support education, and awareness of HIV/AIDS education and prevention.

The 2003 camp offered special significance to NBA stars Marko Jaric, Bostjan Nachbar, and Nikoloz Tskitishvili. Each played with professional teams in Italy prior to the 2002-03 NBA season.

"I am very happy to be taking part in this event that brings together children from across Europe," said Jaric. *"I have great memories from my playing days in Italy, and I would like to share my experiences with the young players. I know they can learn a great deal from me and from the other basketball players taking part."*

National Basketball Association Read to Achieve

Supported by NBA, Women's National Basketball Association, and National Basketball Development League teams, Read to Achieve is a year-round program that encourages youth to develop a life-long love for reading. Reaching an estimated 50 million children a year, Read to Achieve includes annual donations of more than 350,000 books and one million literature magazines through a variety of reading events and book fairs. There are also essay contests and on-line programs available.

The program encourages families and adults to read to young children on a regular basis. Each team and league are committed by using players as spokespeople and provide a "Coaches' Handbook" as a guide to reading with kids.

The Coaches' Handbook lists a number of reasons to read together, questions to ask while reading, and an example of the process.

For example:
- Setting aside at least 15 minutes each day to read aloud
- Rotating the read-aloud responsibility and give every one a turn
- Choosing books that appeal to a child's interest
- Interactive reading
- Using a list of questions before and after reading, such as, why did you choose this book?
- Maintain a reading log

Over 80 Reading Corners and Reading and Learning Centers were created throughout North America. The support of long-time national partners has helped provide access to reading materials and technology. All-Star Reading Teams are comprised of current and former NBA and WNBA players, their families, coaches, trainers, officials, broadcasters, civic leaders, and celebrities, who promote reading efforts through in-arena events, public service announcements, and community appearances. Among the 2002-2003 All-Stars were Jason Terry, Jalen Rose, Penny Taylor, Juwan Howard, Sheryl Swoopes, Isiah Thomas, Jason Kidd, Grant Hill, Yolanda Griffith, Vince Carter, Freddie Prinze, Jr., Debbie Allen, Vivica Fox, and Bow Wow.

The Read to Achieve program offers a bonding experience and a platform to share ideas and information. If reading coaches agree to read to a child every day, they should stick to their promise. The NBA, its teams, and players recognize how critical reading is to future success of every young person.

National Hockey League Diversity Program

The NHL has several minority hockey players including Paul Kariya, Jarome Iginla, Anson Carter, Mike Grier, Georges Laraque, Peter Worrell, Jamie Storr, Richard Park, Joe Juneau, Scott Gomez, Raffi Torres, Sandy McCarthy, Fred Brathwaite, and Chris Simon.

Willie O'Ree headmans NHL Diversity and is the first black hockey player to have played in the league. The program introduces kids of diverse ethnic backgrounds to the game of hockey. The goal is to teach hockey and other life skills to economically disadvantaged children of all ages, creating a fun experience.

Founded in 1995, NHL Diversity offers support and unique programming to youth hockey organizations across North America that are committed to offering economically disadvantaged kids of all ages the opportunity to play hockey. Over 30 inner city volunteer organizations, in various stages of development, have been helped. Over 30,000 kids were exposed to unique hockey experiences. The assistance provided isn't monetary. NHL Diversity provides support in other ways.

Willie O'Ree All-Star Game: Players are selected to play in an east/west game based on citizenship, academics, and dedication to hockey.

Annual NHL Diversity Leadership Meetings: Youth hockey directors are given an opportunity to share their experiences.

The NHL Diversity Equipment Bank: New and used equipment, donated by general public and hockey manufacturers, is delivered to at-risk youths involved in the Diversity program.

Network of professionals: Expertise is offered to help organizations grow.

NHL Diversity ambassadors, Jarome Iginla, Anson Carter, and Kevin Weekes are among those who offer support through street and ice hockey demonstrations and instructional clinics.

"There were only six teams in the league when I broke in and now there are 30 teams," says O'Ree. *"There are about 17 blacks and 37 minority players. It is increasing and it's going to help the game.*

"When I stepped onto the ice on January 18, 1958 in Montreal, I was no stranger to the Montreal fans. I played junior against the Canadien juniors and with the Quebec Aces. When I stepped on the ice that evening, there was no big deal made about it. We beat the Canadiens 3-0, and the big write-up was, "Bruins shutout Habs 3-0". It wasn't until I came back in 1961 that the media gave me the name of "the Jackie Robinson of hockey".

"There were a lot of racial remarks. I had set my goal that I wanted to play in the National Hockey League and whatever I had to do to stay there, I did. It was tough at the beginning. The Bruin organization was behind me 100 percent. The players were very supportive. I just went out and played hockey. I was very happy that I had the opportunity to come up and play with the Bruins. I'm still a Bruin fan."

On Jarome Iginla winning the NHL scoring race in 2001-2002:
"It was a very special moment for me. It was just a nice feeling to know that I had a small part in breaking down barriers and opening doors for players of color that are now playing in the league.

"The players today are bigger and stronger. As far as conditioning, there are better facilities now. There's really no off-season for these players. Once the Stanley Cup finals are over, they may take a week off and they're right into the grind. The one difference from when I played, we played hockey for six months and then we went home and worked at a job for six months. We came to training camp to get into shape. Now these players, when they come to camp, they're already in shape.

"This is my fifth year with NHL Diversity. I've come in contact with so many boys and girls in the cities that I travel. We're giving them an opportunity to play a sport that they never played before. All they need to do is bring themselves. We supply all the equipment and it only costs about $30 a year for these kids to play. You take a family that has three children...it costs about $100, whereas if you

outfitted three boys and girls at a pro shop, it would cost you probably $3,000. That's the one nice thing about the program. The program is working and our logo is "hockey is for everyone". It seems to be mushrooming around the country...giving these boys and girls the opportunity to play."

O'Ree was on hand to provide on-ice assistance to Jarome Iginla when he launched his inaugural hockey school in Calgary as part of the Diversity program in 2002.

"Willie is a legend in hockey. It's a huge honor to have him out at my first hockey school. When I was younger, being a minority and a black player on my team, I looked in the NHL and knew there weren't many black players in the league, but it meant a lot to me to be able to see Grant Fuhr winning Stanley Cups, Claude Vilgrain scoring 30 goals, Tony McKegney - 40. It meant a lot to me back then to know it was possible. As far as me being a role model, it would be a huge honor to be like those guys were to me when I was younger.

"The first message to the kids is to have fun. A lot of times it's a little too serious for the young kids. I was very fortunate my parents were always positive. Whether or not I had a bad game, they were always very positive and realized it was for fun. The kids want to learn.

"The NHL's Diversity initiative has been great and sponsored six scholarships for our entries. The kids had to write an essay and explain why they wanted to be at the camp. I read some of the essays. It was great to see the kids writing and know that they love the game. It was also touching. There were some very good essays. It was a very tough decision. I don't know which six they were. We didn't want to bring attention to them, rather just have them come out and enjoy themselves with the rest of the kids and participate."

Hockey It Pays

IT PAYS is an acronym for I Teach Positive Attitudes in Youth Sports. The brainchild of Dan Bylsma, and his father Jay, it's a program that promotes fun in hockey. It focuses on developing athleticism, an understanding of the game, and using the game to teach life lessons. Among those involved are coaches from Mites to Juniors, doctors, lawyers, psychologists, sports writers, plus mothers and fathers of players from all over North America. The purpose is to provide a wholesome environment for youth to enjoy and grow in the sport of ice hockey. It doesn't conflict with any of the programs established by USA Hockey or Hockey Canada. Instead, it complements them.

The program was started because youth sports, and ice hockey in particular, have developed a reputation for well-publicized incidents of verbal abuse, cheating, beatings, sexual assaults, and homicides. Because of it, kids leave the sport. Attracting and keeping referees becomes increasingly difficult. IT PAYS is an attempt to give players and parents, who have the game in proper perspective, a majority voice to help clean up the sport's reputation.

IT PAYS uses the Internet to report and track the behavior of teams, players, and coaches. Before a team agrees to play in a tournament, it can look up the behavior record of the teams it will be playing.

Each participating team is required to have a National Reporting System administrator. That person takes the responsibility to assess the opposing team for each game. He or she will have access to the IT PAYS database for either input or retrieval. Data is also accessible in summary form to anyone with an interest in seeing the team's record. The information is broken down to that of the players, coaches, and parents.

"You don't want to hear your kids yell at the ref a lot," adds Bylsma. *"Our hope is that the Internet, and it being out for public view, does two things. If I want to, I can steer away from a team I don't want to play. Why? Not because they're good. It's the parents, the coach, or the way the kids behave. Also, it's a way for a team to monitor its own coach and own parents. You can say to your parents, look, we have a bad rating because you're screaming and yelling at the ref, so we'd like you to stop so we don't get a bad rating. You can also monitor your own team, your own coach, and players in the system.*

"On the Internet, we've also tried to add positive incentives to the program. The Los Angeles Kings are doing it. The Anaheim Mighty Ducks are doing it. A few minor league teams are doing it. In all those areas, teams that are doing well, get tickets to a hockey game and come down to the dressing room to see the guys. There's a tournament scheduled by the Kings and the Ducks at the end of the hockey season for teams with the best rating. It has nothing to do with wins or losses. The teams with the best positive sportsmanship are invited to the tournament. We're trying to get a game nationally - to have the teams in Minnesota, Michigan, and Pennsylvania - even teams from out West. We can essentially have a sportsmanship tournament. We're trying to make it a positive program instead of underlining the negative things that seem to be happening (in hockey).

"No one notices the quiet parents. The only people they notice are the one or two people screaming and yelling. Two people give it a bad name. We try to inspire positive behavior with rewards so that positive attitude and respect is prevalent in the game, and the negative stuff just kind of goes away."

Hockey Canada Initiation Program

Hockey Canada recognizes a player's first taste of hockey is crucial. If a beginner has fun, develops some basic skills, and builds self-confidence, there is a good chance they will want to further their hockey.

The Initiation Program's philosophy includes:

- Provide a safe environment to introduce the fundamental skills of ice hockey.
- Develop an understanding of basic teamwork through participation in structured activities and adapted game-like situations.
- Introduce participants to the concepts of fair and co-operative play.
- Refine basic motor patterns and build self-confidence.
- Provide an environment that positively challenges individuals and rewards them for their efforts.
- Provide opportunities to experience a number of activities related in building a lifestyle of fitness and activity.

Designed for five to nine-year-old players, the Initiation Program is about a positive environment to help young athletes grow and develop. Its goal is also to introduce parents to minor hockey, exposing them to what tasks are needed to run a successful program in the hopes that they will become volunteers and keep a long association with the sport.

Corey McNabb oversees the Hockey Canada Initiation Program. *"We really didn't have anything in place in the curriculum for coaches to teach young players the skills of the game. We had a lot of stuff based on coaches, volunteers, or dads who coached based on their own experience growing up. It was deemed that we needed something to make sure the skills of the game are being taught with proper progression, but also in the way that kids are going to have fun and enjoy it.*

"The pilot was launched in Cranbrook, B.C. We had writers who came together and said, "This is what we think the skills are, what we think the progressions are, and this is a realistic way of teaching it." It looked all right in theory, but then it was time to put it to work. Each year, it expanded to more associations. Coincidentally, out of the first program, there were four kids who made the NHL. It's generally unheard of that four kids from one area would make it. Obviously there is coincidence, but a lot of it had to do with the fact that this program was developed and these kids went through it.

"The entire goal of the program is to teach the basic skills, fair play, introduce a team atmosphere, and work together. In 1995, it was put into Hockey Canada's constitution that every minor hockey association had to have the Initiation Program. That's not saying you had to follow it exactly as it is in the manual, but you had to have the program or a plan in place to develop the skills of the players. It's fine to put that mandate into place, but no one really considered that you had to actually have people going into every rink in Canada to police it, which realistically, is almost impossible. We believed this program was so good that people would follow it on their own. I would say 20 percent of the associations follow it very, very well. Another 20 percent follow the basic philosophy. There are probably 40 percent who know what it is and have some sort of development in place. And there are 20 percent who don't follow it at all.

"For example, if I called Calgary Minor Hockey and asked how many of their associations run the Initiation Program, they would say, all of our coaches take the Initiation Clinic, therefore, we think they're running the program. But that's not what happens. Coincidentally, Calgary Minor Hockey is starting (in 2003-04) to put the effort in to have a mandatory following of the Initiation Program for kids aged five and six. They are basically going to say, there are no formal games anymore because they're getting carried away. They complete that by saying, no referees are going to do those games. If you play five on five, full ice, you're not

*having a referee. Therefore, if you do not have a referee as a
sanctioned game, there's no insurance coverage.*

*"There are all kinds of things you can do. It's for the betterment
for the game in the long run and for keeping kids in the game. The
better you are at something, the more apt you are to play, and the
longer you're apt to stay involved.*

*"We have a lot of kids that join at age five and six. If they don't
learn the skills at that age and then all of a sudden, they come into
a situation where they start to play formal games, they're not
involved in the play. They don't get the puck. They never get to
shoot. They'll say, "This isn't all it's cracked up to be. I think I'll
try snowboarding or something else."*

*"The other thing - winning is not the focus, but it's the result.
There are a lot of associations around the country who run the
Initiation Program very well. It just so happens that when their
teams get to be Pee Wee, Bantam, or Midget, they are very
successful. They win most of their games. They win the
championships. They attribute it back to their kids being better
skaters, passers, puck handlers, and better thinkers. As they get
older, the basic skills come natural to them. They don't have to
think about that. They can think about actually playing the game
versus thinking about making a pass.*

*"A branch like the Thunder Bay, Ontario area - they only have
6,000 players in the entire region. They won back-to-back Bantam
championships, back-to-back Midget championships. Based just
on numbers, there's no way a team from (a large city like) Calgary
should play a team from Thunder Bay...the game shouldn't even be
close. They did it back-to-back. They beat all the best teams in
Canada. They went back to the fact that they started the Initiation
Program when those players first started. They learned how to
skate, pass, and shoot, and they did it in a fun atmosphere. All
those kids stayed in the game.*

"When you look at it, it's not rocket science. But parents want to win at eight years old, at nine, and at ten years old. They don't realize the process. That if you go about it the right way, you have a better chance being successful.

"The sort of the philosophy we try to promote about the Initiation Program is that winning and losing is not important. If you go about everything the right way, winning is going to be the result. You're going to get what you want in the end.

"When parents put their kids into swimming or piano lessons, they don't throw them out onto a stage in front of 5,000 people and have them play the piano right away. It takes years to learn the basics. For whatever reason, in hockey, they think if a kid has talent at six or seven years old, they need to be playing games, games, games. Whereas you need to practice, practice, practice, and work on the things you need to improve. It's going to be very hard to change.

"Regarding other countries, we have ten times as many skilled ten year olds. Because of our focus on winning, a skilled ten-year-old player gets turned into a skilled ten-year-old checker, or they get to the red line and dump the puck in. They get the puck in their own zone. They dump it out. They are taught and coached to make the easy plays. Heaven forbid, a coach has a losing record and he's not allowed to volunteer the next year. This is a reality in a lot of places. Parents want to win. Coaches want to win. The end result is, players slow down their development. As they get older, the winning becomes more important.

"We might take a skilled ten year old, who becomes a somewhat skilled 11 year old, and a partially skilled 12 year old. The kids happen to play in a system where it's, stay in your lane, and stay on the right side of the ice. You get to the red line and dump it in. That doesn't take any talent. Anybody can do that. Over time, they lose the ability to be creative and even the willingness to make a

mistake. You're going to learn far more from any mistakes you make than you will from a perfect dump-in. As they get older, especially when they get up to the Western Hockey League or a major junior league, for that coach realistically, it's about winning or he loses his job.

"They coach the players how to win or how to be as successful as they can with the talent they have versus allowing the players to develop more. If you look, for example, at the other countries, they're more focused on the player when they're 18 or 20 versus 16. So they see that 16 to 20 period as very important towards development. They teach very, very few team systems or team play. There's time for that. Who cares if we win a tournament at 14 years old? Their goal is, let's do whatever we can to make these players the best players, and when it comes time to compete for World Juniors or other tournaments, they want their best. The Americans are going through a lot of the same things right now with their basketball program. They didn't win the Worlds so they're re-evaluating a lot of the stuff that's going on.

"Coaches have to be certified, but it's a one-day clinic. You hope that you can give them the philosophy of teaching young kids. It's not about winning or losing. The reality of it is, when you get behind that bench, people want to win. Parents want you to win. It takes a very well rounded coach and a very patient group of parents to allow the best thing to happen for those kids. The coach has to instill in the kids that they want to compete, that they want to try. But you don't have to have the most goals at the end of the game in order to be successful. That's where it takes the well-rounded part of the coach to say, "Last game we lost 10-2, this game we only lost 8-3 - we're getting better." Or "Last time we only completed ten passes, this game we completed 20 passes." You have to find the win in different things versus just the outcome of the game. But unfortunately in our North American society, a lot of times it's the scoreboard at the end.

"I think another place where it probably went wrong was, somewhere along the line, we lost the aspect of free play. We put too much structure in. Part of that is due to technology. Part of it is probably the fault of Hockey Canada in that we have so many resources out there on different aspects of the game. Coaches are trying to teach things to kids - for example, a breakout. The reason a breakout doesn't work is, the kid can't skate. They can't pass or they can't receive a pass. It's not because of a badly planned breakout. It's the execution of it. In some ways, we might have been better if there was never any more information developed, and coaches just let kids play...develop on their own on the outdoor rink, on the pond, learn to discover things, try things. Through television, radio, and the Internet - minor hockey coaches watch the NHL games. They hear the NHL talk about neutral zone traps, this play and that play, and they think, "Hey, I can teach this to my ten year old."

"I would encourage people to look at why Brazil is considered the best soccer country in the world. They don't have any structure. Every single kid plays soccer in the backyard, schoolyard, on the beaches - you name it. They learn the foot skills on their own. Not until they get to a very high level, is when coaches start to implement strategy and how to execute their game plan. The NBA is another perfect example. Most of the guys growing up learn to play basketball in a playground. There were no coaches. They learned by playing. They learned their moves by trying again and again and again. Kobe Bryant was in a commercial where he said, "I learned my skills here", and it shows him in the playground, in the park. "But I perform them here." And they show him in the NBA. That really hit home for me.

"I think one of our problems is, when you get to the Bantam Triple A or Midget Triple A level, those guys have a practice to game ratio which is more practical. The problem is for a lot of them, it's almost too late to go back and learn the fundamentals. Therefore, the teams are concentrating on team play. Whereas, if *we were to reverse that role, by the time they got to Midget Triple A, they would be so much more versed in the fundamental skills of the game.*

"If you can't tell what a team is going to do or what they are doing, then it's a good team because they don't have a set play. Everything seems to be random. They're working on reading and reacting, seeing the ice, and seeing what happens. Teams where you can tell exactly what they're going to do are predictable. They have a lack of skills. They have to take organization and team systems to make up for a lack of skill or a lack of talent.

"There's a coach I know from B.C. who has the worst coaching record of any coach in his league, but he put the most players into NCAA scholarships. He's focusing on developing the players versus the wins."

How does Hockey Canada keep track of everyone in the program?
"We're attempting to do that. I would contact Hockey Alberta and say, "Try to find out how many of your 250 associations are in the Initiation Program." Five years ago they would have said, I don't know. Last year they might have done surveys and said, 150 of them were. Out of those 150, we would be in touch with the ones that do a good job. I'd like to implement a reward system, where every year, each province can put something together. Here's the criteria - we want associations to tell us why they're the best in the Initiation Program and why they should be recognized. The ones that meet the criteria...we reward them, put a big banner in their rink, and do something to recognize their efforts. That can create a lot of positive peer pressure from other associations.

"I'd rather have someone do it because they want to do it and see the benefits rather than, "They told us we had to," and the effort and energy is not there. I don't expect it to be a quick process, but it will happen. It does come down to a funding issue. We have 13 branches so we would try and award 13 winners - at least one per branch.

"If there's a community out there, for whatever reason, produces a lot of players into high level hockey - for example, Cochrane, Alberta. All of a sudden, they get six kids who are drafted into the WHL in the same year. We could start looking at the pattern, check out to see what they do, and interview the coaches. Is it just luck? Natural talent? Did the six kids happen to be born there? Or is there something you do along the way to help them develop it? We just want to share that.

"When Canada started winning the five consecutive world junior medals, in a lot of ways, we probably got complacent. In 1992 to 1997, we won the gold medal five years in a row. Those players would have been 17 and 18. The first year to the fifth year kids would have been exposed to the Initiation Program when they were young. There's probably a correlation there, the fact that these kids got better. I think we got to a point where we were a little bit complacent. We were winning every single year. We didn't really take a good look at what was happening in the rink...what was enabling us to win. The problem started at the first of those five gold medals. In that five-year span, programs got away from the skills development and all of a sudden, we were producing players at 13 to 16 who could not compete with other countries at that level. The problem started long before we actually saw it.

"In reality, other countries are getting better. A lot of that is attributed to our program. The International Ice Hockey Federation bought the rights to the Initiation Program. They view it as a great way to teach hockey to young players. The European countries come over here, see what we do, and take away the best parts of our game, the best parts of their game, and combine it. If we think we're the only country with a passion for hockey, we're wrong. Hockey's the biggest thing going in Finland...the most popular thing in Russia. The Americans are getting bigger and better at it. It's good for the game to have everyone else right at that level.

"Where it has to go - we need to focus on the minor hockey associations. This is our starting point. A lot of associations are at the point where they're saying we need a plan. We can't just let all our coaches do whatever they want to do. The hockey associations are going to say here's a plan. Here are ten different plans based on the number of kids you have...how you can put the Initiation Program to Novice, Atom, Pee Wee, Bantam, and all the way up. I think it's hard for us to expect our kids to be creative if our coaches and we are saying you have to do it this way, at this time, at this point. Let's give them the guidelines and allow them the room to develop. That's almost taking the pond hockey or the outdoor rink and bringing it inside.

"On the national level, I oversee the program. I also have a committee of six people from all over the country. They, in turn, collect data from their region. We basically say this committee sets the agenda for the program. I take everything they have, put it together, and send it back and ask, what do you think? Then I would say it's all up to our branches to implement down to all their hockey associations. In an ideal situation that's what would happen.

"There are some associations that do a great job and others out to find as many games as they can get. It's easier to coach a game than run a good practice. It's pretty easy to tell the next three or five kids they're out next. But to keep 12 or 15 or 30 six year olds entertained on the ice, busy and active, it's not an easy thing. I think the main thing is we have to try and preach patience to the parents."

Hockey Canada's national spokespeople for the Initiation Program are National Hockey League's Paul Kariya and Jayna Hefford of the Canadian Women's Hockey Team.

"Paul Kariya is a perfect example," continues McNabb. *"He learned and perfected so much on his own. He learned in the backyard,*

playing ball hockey. He had a passion for the sport, but he also didn't need it to be totally structured in order for him to enjoy it. He played soccer, baseball, lacrosse - all kinds of different things, which all helped him to become an athlete, not just a hockey player.

"We looked at Paul Kariya for several reasons. Number one, he's a classy individual. He has respect for the game. He has respect for people involved in the game. He has respect for what it takes to stay in the game. I think he plays the game the way it should be played...with speed, finesse, using his skill. I think we need a person like that as a spokesperson to help sell what we're trying to sell in the program. If we went out and got a fighter...people would look at the Initiation Program and say, "Well, we're not sure about that." The same was with Jayna Hefford on the female side. She's the same type of skill player who believes she would not be where she is today if she didn't learn the basic skills.

"Obviously with Paul's NHL schedule, we don't bother him during the season. I ask basically one thing out of him a year - to do a video or photo shoot so we can say, here's our spokesperson. We want a visual for everyone involved in the program. We get some quotes from him - his ideas and thoughts on different things to try and promote that to coaches. He isn't one of those guys to say, here's our ad, here's our program. When we talk to him and ask, "What are your thoughts for developing skills?" He'll say, "Well, I think it's this, this and this." He basically follows the program. That's another reason why we

*Paul
Kariya*

63

have him. If he said, "Aw, I think you ought to play 120 games a year and you don't need to practice." We would have said, "Sorry, we'll look for someone else." His philosophy and thoughts on the game are the same as ours. He'll autograph items like jerseys, sticks, and we'll use that for hockey associations that do a good job with the program - donate the items for a fundraiser or raffle prize. So they see when they follow the Initiation Program, there are some benefits to it. With Jayna it's the same way."

Youth Football Camps

The National Football League, Canadian Football League, and other leagues often make a concerted effort to offer football camps for youth in order to connect with the community while bringing exposure to a game some kids may not have the opportunity to play. These camps focus on the basic skills from passing, kicking, blocking, and defense. Camps can be one day, a few days, or a week in length. Drills may be non-contact or tackle but most instruction comes from professional football players and other local football personnel.

Pass, Punt, and Kick football camps target boys and girls from as young as six to high school age. They get an opportunity to compete amongst a group in punting, passing, and place kicking. Every participant receives the same number of repetitions. In a national program, top scorers in all age divisions may advance to another round of competition or receive prizes. The logistics will vary from camp to camp. In a professional league-driven camp, the top performers may have an opportunity to show their skills and play in a final competition at a league stadium either pre-game or halftime.

The NFL has also launched a youth tackle program for boys 12 to 14 where participants learn step-by-step instruction on every position from professional players who team up with high school coaches. The program also offers life skills and character development.

Baseball Tomorrow Fund

It's a joint initiative between Major League Baseball and the Major League Baseball Players Association. Its mission is to promote and enhance the growth of baseball globally. The Baseball Tomorrow Fund provides financial assistance to programs, fields, and equipment purchases so youth are afforded an opportunity to participate in baseball or softball.

Grants are flexible in order to address the individual needs of a community. For example, neighborhoods might need to finance a new program, expand or improve an existing program, undertake a new collaborative effort, or obtain facilities or equipment. The fund doesn't act as a substitute for existing funding or fundraising activities and it can't be used for recurring building maintenance or operating costs or construction.

There is a long list of those who have benefited from the program. One recipient organization was able to provide free youth baseball clinics to over 1,000 kids in two states. The fund also helped them continue and expand the program, and they were able to purchase additional equipment. Another group received funds to establish a new softball team that gave at-risk teens an opportunity to play. The Baseball Tomorrow Fund also helped renovate a youth baseball field for a new-formed Little League.

The bottom line of the program is to connect kids with baseball and softball to enrich their lives individually and that of their communities.

Reviving Baseball in Inner Cities

Another initiative sponsored by Major League Baseball, the Reviving Baseball in Inner Cities (RBI) program helps promote the game to teenage boys and girls who live in disadvantaged neighborhoods. The RBI also partners with the Boys and Girls Clubs of America.

Former Major League player, John Young, founded the program in 1989 in South Central Los Angeles, his childhood neighborhood. As a kid, Young observed a significant decrease in the number of skilled athletes from inner city locations. The RBI program was initiated to help youth overcome the obstacles of lack of funding, community support, lack of organization, and street gangs that ultimately prevent disadvantaged kids from learning the game. He also wanted to help them combat academic and social disadvantages.

Major League Baseball provided financial support and readily endorsed the program. After enough equipment and fields were gathered to field 24 teams, Young helped create the Academy of Excellence Program as a supplement to the RBI.

Located at Santa Monica College, the Academy of Excellence Program assesses the academic performance of Los Angeles RBI participants. It provides for individual tutoring, college and SAT preparation courses, and even helps kids with goal setting and time management. The Academy's top student receives the Bart Giamatti Award, named after MLB's former Commissioner.

The RBI program soon spread to other major league ports, among others, and is now administered by MLB. The league has amassed over $15 million worth of resources to carry it forward. RBI coaching seminars include topics from life skills, baseball skills, conflict resolution, media training, marketing, and fundraising. In its effort to promote an interest in baseball, it also raises the self-esteem of disadvantaged children and encourages them to stay in school thus stay off the streets. Over 120,000 youth in 185 cities worldwide have benefited from the program.

Chapter 4

Role Models

Shareef Abdur-Rahim

National Basketball Association Forward
Future Foundation *www.future-foundation.com*

He was the third overall pick in the 1996 NBA Draft. Basketball star,
Shareef Abdur-Rahim launched the Future Foundation as a way to
help at-risk kids access the fundamental skills they need to survive
in today's world. A human network of partners, employees, and
volunteers, the Future Foundation teams up with organizations, such
as The Atlanta Hawks Foundation, Children's Restoration Network,
Our House, Atlanta Children's Shelter, and Teens at Work. The
Foundation also provides for scholarships at Wheeler High School
at Abdur-Rahim's hometown of Marietta, Georgia.

The Future Foundation spearheaded construction on the "Reef
House", which takes on Abdur-Rahim's nickname "Reef", a facility
that provides after school programs for elementary school children.
Besides housing a computer lab and recreation room, Reef House
offers mentoring and tutoring, plus classes in arts and crafts,
physical education, and theatre.

Abdur-Rahim helps feed disadvantaged people in the Atlanta area
through the "Rebound Against Hunger" program. For every
rebound he grabs during the course of a season, Future Foundation
and sponsoring partners donate $25 to the Atlanta Community
Food Bank.

Abdur-Rahim hosts several annual events. The "Back to School
Rally" is a day of games, prizes, music, and more. Backpacks and
after school supplies are donated to hundreds of Atlanta youth.
Abdur-Rahim and volunteers from the Future Foundation deliver

complete turkey dinners to over 1,800 people in the Atlanta area for the Thanksgiving Turkey Delivery. The "Shareef for Kids" program collects toys for disadvantaged children and Abdur-Rahim personally delivered the first load to the Atlanta Children's Shelter.

Abdur-Rahim participated in many other charitable events - all within the same year. Among them were the annual Atlanta Hawks Foundation Golf Classic (benefiting the Hawks Foundation), The Hawks Tip-Off Luncheon (benefiting the Hawks Foundation), with his teammates - visiting the Salvation Army Boys and Girls Club to deliver free turkeys and play games with the kids, and hosting over 50 disadvantaged youth from the Georgia Department of Human Resources at the Hawks Holiday Bowling Party. Hall of Famer, Bob Lanier, joined Abdur-Rahim and WNBA star, Nykesha Sales, for the unveiling of a newly refurbished basketball court at the Anderson Boys and Girls Club in Marietta, Georgia, during NBA All-Star 2003 as part of the NIKE Reuse-A-Shoe program. He visited a group of terminally and critically ill children with their families at a special send off breakfast before the group departed for Disney World.

Ray Allen

National Basketball Association Guard
"Ray of Hope" Foundation

His mandate is to offer hope for children. Allen's "Ray of Hope" Foundation provides food and clothing for the disadvantaged among other needs. The Foundation was established as a way to give back to the children of Hartford, Connecticut. It also marshals basketball clinics and supports other community organizations.

This NBA All-Star has raised monies for Special Olympics, the American Diabetes Association, Mayor Mike's Companies for Kids, and his own foundation through the Connecticut Classic, a charity basketball game. The Ray Allen Night Classic at Hartford's Goodwin Park benefits The First Tee of Hartford youth golf program.

Allen is a member of the All-Star Advisory Council for the Junior NBA and Junior WNBA youth basketball support program. The group provides no cost assistance to qualified recreational youth basketball leagues serving boys and girls age five to 14.

Allen is the NBA Spokesman for the Thurgood Marshall Scholarship Fund and, with other players, has donated blocks of tickets to local non-profit organizations for NBA home games.

Shawn Bradley

National Basketball Association Center

Bryan's House and The Rise School of Dallas are two organizations that Shawn Bradley champions. Bryan's House is a managed-care facility for children whose lives are affected by HIV and AIDS. It focuses on the family unit as being an integral part of a healthy life. The Rise School of Dallas provides instruction to children with Down's syndrome between 18 months and six years of age.

Bradley offers his support through charitable gifts from his Dunk Shot and Block Shot promotions. Fifty dollars per activity are matched with Dunk Shot funds to bolster financing for The Rise School. Those gifts have totaled $16,000 in the past two years alone. Bryan's House is the beneficiary of Block Shot funds totaling $35,000 in two seasons. On October 9, 2002, Shawn took part in the dedication of the first Dallas Mavericks/IBM Learning Center in Dallas, located at Bryan's House.

As the national spokesman for the Children's Miracle Network, Bradley partakes in their annual telethon each June. He also acts as a spokesman for Jingle Balls, a program that encourages the public to donate sporting goods to help out needy youth.

From May 1991 to May 1993, Bradley completed a two-year church mission in Sydney, Australia, before entering the NBA Draft. He was picked second overall by the Philadelphia 76ers in 1993.

Dan Bylsma

National Hockey League Right Wing
Hockey It Pays www.hockeyitpays.com
www.danbylsma.com

Over the years, he received a lot of feedback from parents while operating a hockey school in Grand Rapids, Michigan. Couple that with his research on four books and Dan Bylsma discovered the idea of promoting positive behavior in youth hockey through a website. The checking NHL winger consulted with his father, Jay, who helped him brainstorm concepts that led to IT PAYS. Bylsma and his dad co-authored, "So Your Son Wants To Play in the NHL" and "So You Want To Play in the NHL", among two other books on youth sports.

While he earns his living with a hockey stick, Bylsma learned early that other things were more important than sports. *"I had three other brothers. Playing sports was something my parents offered us as a prize for doing the things that were required of us. Like schoolwork, eating your vegetables, going to church, youth group on Wednesday night. Sports were the things we got to do because we followed the rules of the household. If you didn't eat your vegetables, you got to watch your brothers and sisters go out in the backyard and play hockey while you sat and stared at a plate of carrots and peas you didn't want to eat. Eventually, no matter how bad you didn't like them, you ate your vegetables because you couldn't stand them playing in the backyard. It was a way for our parents to tell us what was important to them. We missed some hockey games on Sunday to go to*

Dan Bylsma

church. Occasionally we missed church to play hockey games when a game was deemed important enough, like a tournament. More often, we rearranged the hockey game to go to church. I knew in the long run that my parents thought that church was far more important than playing a sport. I knew that school was far more important than playing a sport.

"Sports turned out to be something I really wanted to do, and I really wanted to do well. Not because my parents wanted it or that I was getting pressure to do it. That's what made my parents think I was a good kid. If I did well in school, I got praise from my parents. Going to church and doing well, I got praise from my parents. Sports were something I wanted to do.

"I don't mean to belittle the experience you can have in sports. It's a great opportunity for kids to learn life lessons. It's a great opportunity to be able to understand that if you scream and yell at the referee there are consequences. If you break the rules, you're going to the penalty box. That correlates to what we have in life. You get in trouble with the law...there are penalties for that. In winning and losing in life, there are so many losses in life - so many ups and so many downs. Hockey is just like that. You win. You lose. You have ups and downs with your coaches, your teammates. You have injuries. All those things are parallels to life. Those things can help you be a thriving adult. That's why I think the game is so great. For people who play sports, there's a chance to get them ready for life. You can play hockey for a living and that's great, but there are also so many other things to do. You may choose to be a teacher...anything, and the lessons you learn in the sports arena, are what you are going to take with you to cope with things as an adult. That's what sports can be.

"Having said that, there is a negative side. There can be negative influences. If you're taught that cheating is okay at the nine-year-old level, then cheating might be okay to you at the 22-year-old level. It's a microcosm of life. It's a chance for us as adults and parents to teach kids what they might expect in life.

"When we start to lose respect of our sports, you're setting kids up for a difficult time in life. Hockey's great and it's a huge part of my life. It's not the be-all end-all. If I fail at hockey or I didn't make it at hockey, it doesn't mean I'm not going to be a successful person. When we put everything in hockey, at the sake of everything else in your life, you're setting yourself up for failure. Even if you're successful in hockey, if you're in the NHL or not, you're still setting yourself up for failure.

"The fact that eight out of 10 NHL players may do something positive - no one really writes about that. It's not news. If you do something good, no one might hear about it. If someone goes to a school or makes a visit every other week to a hospital, we don't really want that out in public, but it's not that big of a story. It's only a big story if a player has a bad night.

"I really do believe that there's no difference in people in hockey than there is at work, in school, or somewhere else. They all do bad things. There are people in hockey that do bad things. We're not exclusive to that. We don't have a corner on the market. I understand the media sensationalizes it and people read about it. I don't let it bother me because there's nothing I can do about it. Can we not talk about it? It's not doing any good. There are a ton of athletes who have done a ton of good for amateur hockey. Talk about the good people.

"If there's any problem in minor hockey, it's an adult problem and not a kid problem. If the kids are emulating the NHL players, it's because the parents are letting them. Kids aren't stupid. If you say to them, you see what so and so did in the game, we're not allowed to do that. It's not acceptable. If you do that, you will sit on the end of the bench. Every kid understands that pretty clear. But more often than not, the parents want those things to come out. They know they need to be aggressive, to be physical. They know they're going to have to fight. That's what adults talk about. I get people asking a question quite often. Kids are about eight, nine, or 10 years old and they say, the kid's a good hockey player, he goes in

the corner but when someone hits him, he shies away. I'd like him to be a little more aggressive. How do I do that? They're talking about a nine-year-old kid. The first time I got this question, I said to the father, if you want your nine-year-old to be more aggressive and be more violent, then you should beat him. If you want him to be respectful, play within the rules, don't worry about it. He's nine and he'll get his testosterone later. He'll figure out when he's 14...when someone hits him, you don't run away. You know you can hit back. Paul Kariya hit me. He's got the puck. I get to hit him. That's how hockey's played. When the parents say - I want them to be more aggressive. I say to them the same answer every time - beat your kid. If you want him to be really aggressive, beat him for no reason. He'll be aggressive. Talk about being hungry for the puck and going to the net. Those are things you can inspire your kid to do. I think we're trying to get our kids to emulate professional athletes.

"When I played junior and community hockey. The rule in my house was, if I got in a fight, my father would personally come and take me off the bench, out of the game, and out of the arena. That started when I was six until I was in Junior B. I could watch fighting with someone on the Detroit Red Wings all I wanted, but I knew that wasn't acceptable."

Vince Carter

National Basketball Association Guard
Embassy of Hope Foundation www.vincecarter15.com

Vince Carter believes it is important to share his accomplishments and good fortune with those who are not so fortunate. That's why he started the Embassy of Hope in 1998. The idea was based on the slogan "Believing in Your Dreams," which represented Carter's lifelong commitment to perseverance and achievement.

Each month, Carter provides tickets to Raptors' home games for "Vince's Hoop Group" - students from the Nelson A. Boylan

Collegiate Institute, where he makes special visits. Students are chosen as members of the Hoop Group based on their commitment to self-improvement through academics and community work. Carter then meets with them after each game and engages them in conversation on how a good education can help overcome obstacles.

Carter and his mother, Michelle, played Santa to 15 families from a Toronto shelter at a "Believing in Christmas" party, an Embassy of Hope Foundation initiative. Children and their mothers lunched with the NBA star and spent the afternoon opening gifts.

The Vince Carter Wheelchair Basketball Clinic is an extension of the Vince Carter Youth Basketball Academy. The free basketball clinic welcomed 42 wheelchair athletes in a half-day basketball clinic and mini basketball tournament on September 22, 2002. Carter presented a motivational talk addressing four key principles - Vision, Teamwork, Adversity, and Balance and answered questions from the audience. At the clinic's conclusion, players, coaches, and volunteers were treated to a lunch and personally received a gift bag from Carter.

Basketball instruction is provided to kids from age eight to 18 through The Vince Carter Youth Basketball Academy. Participants at the four-day camp are taught fundamental skills and the team concept of basketball. There is also an educational component incorporated into each daily session. The Vince Carter Youth Basketball Academy hosted 750 kids in 2002.

The Bell Raptorball Youth Leagues (BRBYL) promotes the development of basketball in Canada to which Carter is the national spokesman. The BRBYL Open Practice gathers participants, coaches, and volunteers to attend an NBA practice and receive a chance to win an opportunity to play basketball with Carter at the Air Canada Center. About 30,000 youth have entered the BRBYL program.

Carter took part in the Raptors Foundation King Pin Challenge, a bowling event giving fans a chance to bowl with the team and raise money for Toronto children's charities. He visits hospitals to offer words of encouragement, sign autographs and photos. He is involved with the Rap Up Charity (benefiting Toronto children's charities), the NBA Read to Achieve program, and donated $2.5 million dollars to his alma mater, Mainland High School in Daytona Beach, Florida, to finance enhancements for a new gymnasium. The new gymnasium, slated to open in the spring of 2005, will be named the Vince Carter Athletic Centre.

The Vince Carter Summer Jam is a series of charity events hosted by Carter, which includes the Vince Carter Charity All-Star Game, the Vince Carter All-Star Charity Golf Classic, and the Vince Carter Youth Basketball Academy. Funds raised exceeded 2002's goals by $100,000 to the tune of approximately $450,000.

Tyson Chandler

National Basketball Association Forward

Tyson Chandler helps real-life people in real-life situations. He contributed $10,000 to pay the gas bills for Chicago families unable to afford to heat their homes or purchase smoke detectors. Peoples Gas utility company and the mayor's office helped identify which families were in need and administered the funds.

With Chicago Bulls head coach, Bill Cartwright, Chandler supported a Chicago Firemen's Association campaign to educate homeowners about the importance of smoke detectors. Both were depicted in advertising campaign photos wearing firefighter attire, spreading the message that smoke detectors can save lives.

Chandler routinely makes unsolicited visits to children and fans who are handicapped, sick, guests of charity sections, or who might appreciate the special attention of an NBA player prior to each pre-game warm up. He not only says hello and takes photos, but he engages them in a complete conversation.

With the Read to Achieve program, Chandler hosted the arts and crafts section at the season launch in October 2002 and assisted with literacy activities at the team's annual Holiday Party where over 100 children attended. He recorded public service announcements for the Bulls, co-hosted the Post-Run Party for a Bulls fundraiser, and makes frequent visits to children's homes and hospitals.

Chandler shuns personal recognition for his charitable efforts. Regardless, his charismatic personality draws fans of all ages to this very young star.

Michael Curry

National Basketball Association Forward

It started out as a canned food drive to benefit one Thanksgiving but an overwhelming response led Michael Curry to continue the drive through three Piston home games the following month. The items were donated to inner city Detroit's Capuchin Soup Kitchen. Curry purchased toys for his Curry Canned Food Drive and Toy Exchange to trade for each food item dropped off at St. Rita's Catholic Church on Detroit's eastside. The Detroit Rescue Mission, which provides food and services for families and individuals in need, received all of the nonperishable food items.

With teammate Tayshaun Prince, Curry read books to over 50 children from the Guest Boys and Girls Club of Dearborn, Michigan. Thanks to a partnership with sponsors, Curry and Prince took three lucky winners a shopping spree for the Boys and Girls Club at the reading event's conclusion.

Voted the NBA's Community Assist winner in December 2002, Curry recorded public service announcements focusing on the importance of reading in children's daily lives. He is an active Read to Achieve participant.

Dale Davis

National Basketball Association Center/Forward
The Dale Davis Foundation

Each home game, Dale Davis donates tickets to the Blazers community ticket program. He has his own record label - World Ain't Right (WAR) and his Dale Davis Foundation benefits at-risk and economically disadvantaged youth.

Literacy is at the heart of much of his volunteer work. A member of the NBA's All-Star Reading Team, Davis is also a Verizon literacy champion for SMART, a nonprofit program that connects volunteers with Oregon children who need one-on-one reading support. He supports the Multnomah County Library's Everybody Reads program through volunteer reading. Davis surprises students with gifts, toys, and clothing for the Blazers' Albina Head Start adopted classrooms, and started a $10,000 Portland scholarship that high school seniors can use towards college or university.

Davis personally brightened Christmas for over 100 families by collecting food to distribute to an entire neighborhood in need as part of his first annual Food Drive and Giveaway.

Vlade Divac

National Basketball Association Center
Group7/Divac Children's Foundation

The Serbia-Montenegro native never played college basketball, but Vlade Divac put five professional seasons under his belt, playing in his home country before joining the Los Angeles Lakers in 1989. He was only 12 years old when he left home to play and only 16 when he signed his first professional contract.

The "Divac Fund" through the St. John Foundation was started to help children affected by the war in Yugoslavia. The first

Charita-Bowl" celebrity bowling fundraiser tallied almost
$70,000 for the Divac Children's Foundation, Group 7, and for the
Sacramento Children's Home. The Group 7/Divac Children's
Foundation was launched in 1995 with fellow Yugoslavian players
Predrag Danilovic, Aleksandar Djordjevic, Zarko Paspalj,
Zeljko Rebraca, Dejan Bodiroga, and Zoran Savic.

Divac visits with cancer patients, foreign exchange students, and
at-risk youth after games. He and his father have distributed food,
Christmas trees, and decorations to over 40 families. Divac also
hosts summer basketball camps that benefit charity. He is directly
involved with the United Nations' International Drug Campaign, is
a UNICEF spokesperson, and attended Basketball without Borders.

He is a Hometown Hero Award recipient (2001) and received the
2000 J. Walter Kennedy Citizenship Award.

Tim Duncan

National Basketball Association Forward/Center
The Tim Duncan Foundation

The Tim Duncan Foundation was founded in 2001 to serve the San
Antonio, Winston-Salem, and the U.S. Virgin Islands in support of
health awareness and research, education, youth sports and
recreation. The Tim Duncan Bowling for Dollar$ Charity
Bowl-A-Thon and the Slam Duncan Charity Golf Classic are
annual events that raise money for the foundation. Duncan has
distributed over $450,000 towards Breast and Prostate Cancer
detection, prevention, and research.

The Tim Duncan Foundation Charity Golf Classic was launched in
2003 at the La Cantera Palmer Course in San Antonio. Over
$60,000 was raised for community programs. The Tim Duncan
Character Champions program, also started in 2003, recognizes
children who demonstrate integrity, respect, dependability, fairness,
caring, and civic responsibility. At least 3,000 Character Champion

students will earn tickets to Spurs, American Hockey League Rampage, and WNBA games or SeaWorld along with t-shirts and achievement certificates.

Duncan received the NBA's Home Team Community Service Award in 2001 and earmarked $25,000 towards the San Antonio's Children's Shelter for abused, abandoned, and neglected children in Bexar County. Duncan has a degree in psychology from Wake Forest.

Adonal Foyle

National Basketball Association Forward
www.adonalfoyle.com

He grew up on the unassuming island of Canouan and while Adonal Foyal is working on a masters degree in Sports Psychology, the NBA star is a strong advocate for free speech.

He founded a non-partisan organization, Democracy Matters, in 2001 to give students a voice in issues of democracy and encourage activism. Hundreds of students and faculty in over 30 colleges nationwide discuss issues of campaign finance reform. Foyle's goal is for students to develop their leadership skills and thus help deepen the country's democracy. This is done with high school students and local communities through teach-ins, letter writing, petition campaigns, educational seminars, and voter registration drives. Foyle serves as President and Chairman of the Board of Democracy Matters.

The official spokesperson for the Warriors "Tall Tales" Reading program, Foyle is also involved in the "Making the Grade" program, an organization serving to prevent middle school children from dropping out when they reach high school.

Foyle received the NBA's Community Assist Award in 2002.

Lawrence Funderburke

National Basketball Association Forward
Lawrence Funderburke Youth Organization

He is perhaps one of the most active community-minded players on his team's roster. Lawrence Funderburke fully understands the enormous impact he has as a role model and public figure. As a graduate from Ohio State, he also understands the importance of a college education. It's one of the reasons he created the Lawrence Funderburke Youth Organization, Inc (LFYO).

LFYO is committed to providing activities that will enhance the moral, educational, and social development of economically disadvantaged youth. It furnishes positive role models and educational opportunities to youth through after school programs.

More than just implementing a program and saying an occasional hello, Funderburke tries to connect himself personally in students' everyday lives, talk to their parents, and engage them in positive activities. Field trips include ice skating, dinners at formal restaurants, IMAX movies such as "Space Odyssey," museum visits, and trips to local businesses to see first hand the types of jobs available to them.

Funderburke holds a banquet for his students at each season's end when he asks how they are doing. He communicates with their parents over the summer, making sure the skills and knowledge from their studies and field trips are being put to good use. Besides outreaching to the current enrollment, Funderburke maintains ongoing contact with students who participated in the past.

"Continuing in your education to the best of your ability will help you to become a productive person, not only to see the world as a whole, but also to those who deeply love and care about you - your family, your friends and your teachers," says Funderburke. *"I have started the Lawrence Funderburke Youth Organization, Inc. to*

break the mindset of the zero curse game and to introduce the 'plus one, negative zero' campaign."

Besides his own program, Funderburke is involved in numerous team events and programs including TeamUp, Stay in School, and the Kings Reading Challenge. Lawrence and his wife, Monya, have helped prepare and serve over 1,500 meals each year for homeless and welfare families. He co-hosted a school rally in Albuquerque, New Mexico when his team was in town for a preseason game. A $100,000 endowment was established at Ohio State to provide scholarship support for disadvantaged youth attending the Fisher College of Business and other undergraduate programs.

Funderburke was named winner of the NBA's first-ever Hometown Hero of the Month community service award. He received the Ohio State University Fisher College of Business Community Service Award in 2002. Funderburke serves on the Board of the Boys and Girls Club of Columbus, Ohio, and is an All-Star with the Read to Achieve program. He speaks some Spanish and Greek, studies Shorin-Ryu martial arts, and is a finance intern during the summer off-season. He is working toward his Masters in Business Administration, will publish a children's book by 2004, and hopes to own a financial planning company in the near future.

Doug Gilmour

National Hockey League Center/Left Wing

Fans love him. His teammates love him. Even the media loves him. Doug Gilmour is one of those guys who can command attention, even when he has nothing to say. A 20-plus-season veteran, Gilmour is the ultimate hockey hero. Nicknamed "Killer" for his on-ice tenacity, outside the arena, he's one the softest speaking people around.

Is growing up tougher for kids today than when he grew up?
"Obviously that's a tough question. A lot of specialists are looking

into it as well. I think the pressure of society now is much more demanding. I don't know if it's pressure or expectations of whether they should be doing this or doing that. We were just kids. We just played hockey...sports in general at school. It was fun. There were no expectations. The parents made sure you were polite and a good kid. That's how you want your kids to grow up. I don't think we should force our children to do anything or to try to lead them in the right way. They'll make the decisions."

What do you think your life would be like if you were not in sports? *"That's the toughest question anybody's ever asked me because I've never thought about it. I truly believe sports or different clubs for children are where kids can occupy their time...not sit around the house on the computer all the time. Physical activity, in general, is more healthy for them...the spirit and mind as well."*

Gilmour has a daughter just over 18 and two boys six and four. His reaction to his daughter turning 18: *"I had her when I was 10 (laughing). My daughter still plays hockey at high school. She does a number of other activities. My little guy is just getting into it now. As little kids go, they've got a lot of energy, whether its playing soccer or hockey. They're getting to the age now where they're starting to appreciate a lot more sports."*

In looking back at his childhood and sports: *"I remember playing hockey and I had three goals one game. After the game, I put my stuff in the trunk of the car then went out to get it when my dad said, "That stuff is not coming out." I asked, "What do you mean?" He said, "Well, you didn't do anything out there today. You didn't work. Everything came natural for you so forget it, it's staying in there. If you want to go back and play, you take that out and go work* next time." The next game I didn't have any points, came back thinking, what's he going to say now? He said, "Good game." Right there was just a quick lesson that he taught me. Whatever your children might want to be involved in, give it a good effort. Work hard and I truly believe, in life, you'll succeed that way.

"My brother is 13 years older than I am. When I was growing up, he was playing junior hockey with Darryl Sittler and Dan Maloney. I idolized him. I wanted to watch him play hockey. As time went on, you start watching television and your hockey heroes. Bobby Orr was the person foremost. I was a defenseman and used to wear number four...so it was like, number four, Bobby Orr, Doug Gilmour. I thought it rhymed. That's how I worked. As you get older and closer to Junior A, you start thinking you might have a chance to make it. I was also a big follower of Wayne Gretzky...the way he saw the ice and everything else."

On the pressure difference in today's NHL as compared to when first came in: "Yes there is pressure. A lot of times the expectations are there. There shouldn't be as much pressure. It should be about the same. The difference now is, it's a lot more money being made. I broke in 1983 when the highest paid guy on the team was making $400,000. Your goal was to get to that one day. I was 20. There was pressure to make it, but sometimes the money factor steps over the line, more so than the game in general. That's where we've got to figure out the way the game's going to go, where everyone can succeed at it.

"We leave home at 16 years old to go live with a family and play hockey. Then all of a sudden you have a chance to go pro or to the minors. Then all of a sudden, you're on your own. You've got to have good people around you. I've been with my agent for 22 years. It's good people that keep you grounded, but at the same time, they teach you. Now you've got a checking account. You have this, pay your taxes, and everything else.It's a lot different. You learn and hopefully everybody learns the right way and not the hard way."

On so many adverse distractions: *"That's an issue that's brought up in training camp. We can get people checked out now. Years ago, we made mistakes. We did. We gave money to the wrong people and that's something you can't worry about. That's where your agent and other people around you can really help you out. You see somebody from the surrounding area - you say, "I don't think you should be hanging around with that person." It's a quick lesson but that's just a lesson of growing up as well. Hopefully everybody's grounded enough to have that money for years to come for your future after hockey."*

On being a role model: *"Yes, there are children, the same way I grew up, watching different athletes and who they are. I love charity work. That's something that I strongly believe in and will continue doing after I'm done playing. When you look at the role models, I love to see the children's faces, those that are going through certain situations, where you can help them or just put a smile on their face for that one minute of the day, when other days they are in pain and struggling. That's a role model. When you walk into any one of those hospitals and don't feel bad about yourself. You see some kids that are fighting for their lives - it's just not right."*

Brian Grant

National Basketball Association Center
The Brian Grant Foundation www.briangrant44.com

Brian Grant and his wife, Gina, have a wide-reaching impact on a number of communities. They are hands-on in their philanthropic effort to help needy families of all ages.

The Brian Grant Foundation bestows funding to a group of organizations in the South Florida community plus those in his former NBA hometown of Portland. Part of that support entails dinners for families involved with Mothers Against Gang

Violence in Northeast Portland. Grant works closely with underprivileged children and non-supported elderly, residing in local rehabilitation centers.

"Grant's Army" is a community ticket distribution program that enables both socially underprivileged, physically disadvantaged, and health-failing youth to meet members of the Miami HEAT and participate in other in-arena activities. These tickets are donated to numerous Miami charities that include Big Brothers/Big Sisters, Ronald McDonald House, and many other South Florida non-profit organizations. Grant personally visits the arena's "Grant's Army" section after each home game.

The Grants partnered with South Florida's Neighbors 4 Neighbors, purchasing clothing and toys for needy Miami families. They also donated Thanksgiving dinners for residents at a Rescue Mission.

Brian and his wife are co-founders of The Positive Partnership Program, reaching out to public schools by nurturing students with a positive connection to the community. They launched the "Scholastic Attendance Program" in Portland to encourage students to stay in school. They offer tickets to Blazers games as a reward for attending class.

The "Brian's Bash" golf tournament raised over $200,000 for Ronald McDonald House, but Grant also supports numerous other organizations such as Big Brothers/Big Sisters of Miami; United Way of Miami; Hadassah of Miami; Greater Miami Chamber of Commerce; HEAT Academy at Dunbar, Red Cross of South Florida; SAFESPACE; Jackson Memorial Hospital-Guardian Angels, and Children's Home Society. Grant hosts basketball camps and visits hospitals year-round to bring kind words to suffering children and their families.

Allan Houston

National Basketball Association Guard
Allan Houston Charitable Fund www.allanhouston.com

Houston's main passion is mentoring children. *"I'm committed to creating an environment for growth - spiritually, intellectually, emotionally, and where possible, professionally - where youth can nurture their gifts and explore their God-given talents. This is the ultimate goal of my charitable endeavors."*

The Allan Houston Charitable Fund, created with his wife, Tamara, advocates organizations that support, encourage, and impact children. The fund's first gift was $100,000 to the New York City Board of Education's World Trade Center Fund to help it meet the physical and psychological needs of students and schools after the World Trade Center attacks on September 11, 2001.

My Teacher Is My Hero Award was initiated as part of his community service with the Knicks. New York City Public School students are asked to write about a teacher who has had a positive impact on their lives. The award recognizes one teacher from each grade level (elementary, intermediate, and high school). Houston presents the author penning the winning essay and the teacher with the award at halftime. In 2001, over 3,000 students responded.

Allan Houston's Courtside Classroom provides tickets to New York City students for every home game, who are personally met and fed by Houston.

Houston was the recipient of Teen People Magazine's Community Service Award and is the national spokesman for USA Mentoring. He works with the All-Star Weekend's Slammin Jammin Jubilee Clinic, benefiting Christian Athletes United and the Wade Houston Scholarship Award, which provided $25,000 to four African-American students.

Juwan Howard

National Basketball Association Forward
www.juwanhoward.com

He will always remember the streets of Southside Chicago and how frightened he was at the sounds of gunfire keeping him awake at night. A neighborhood filled with violence, drugs, and gangs made it difficult for Juwan Howard to believe he could realize his dreams. It's one of the reasons he founded the Juwan Howard Foundation in 1994. He wanted to offer hope to inner city kids…to allow them to dream of a better future.

Better education, recreational opportunities, moral support, and encouragement—these are the tools the foundation uses to help at-risk kids in a number of inner city communities.

His Warm Hearts Drive has clothed numerous children and adults with over 31,000 articles. Over 2,000 coats were collected for the Denver Rescue Mission alone.

The foundation's Literacy Challenge encourages students to read at least 45 minutes a day. The program, which supports Chicago Public Schools, reaches over 40,000 students. Participants have the opportunity to attend the Juwan Howard Celebrity Basketball Camp and draw for prizes. Howard is also part of the Nuggets All-Star Reading Team in the NBA's Read to Achieve program. He is a national board member of Reading is Fundamental, which develops and delivers children and family literacy programs to promote regular reading.

Other charitable endeavors by Howard include donating $50 for each home game rebound and assist to the Pentagon Relief Fund. He purchases 100 Nugget season tickets and donates them back to underprivileged youth. At Christmas, he has provided gifts to a family residing in a transitional housing facility for single-parent homeless families.

Howard is a recipient of the 2003 Chopper Travaglini Award, given annually to a Nuggets player who best exemplifies the spirit of generosity and dedication to improving the lives of children. As part of the ceremony, Howard donated over $6,000 to the Denver Nuggets Community Fund.

Larry Hughes

National Basketball Association Guard
The Larry Hughes Family Foundation
www.larryhughesfoundation.com

When Justin Hughes received a heart transplant in 1997, it altered the life of his older brother Larry. The Larry Hughes Family Foundation, created by the NBA star and his mother, Vanessa, educates the public about organ donation. The foundation provides funds to create a comfortable environment for families affected by organ transplants - to alleviate the stress of emotional and financial effects. Howard donates his time to the GET GAME-GIVE LIFE campaign, which brings awareness to college students and increases their participation in the transplant initiative - like signing donor cards. His efforts have made him and Justin the recipient of the First Family Pledge Award of Thanks in 2000.

He helps families in other ways too. The Larry Hughes Gas Giveaway pumps 3,000 gallons of gas into Bay Area vehicles. Howard also participates in the Wizards Holiday Foster Care Party for kids.

Jarome Iginla

National Hockey League Right Wing

What you see is what you get. Charismatic, approachable, kind, generous - all these things describe Jarome Iginla, who is fast becoming one of the hottest stars in the National Hockey League. Whenever a team-driven charity function arises, Iginla is there, front and center. He strongly supports the Juvenile Diabetes Foundation and KidSport Calgary. Each year, he participates in a golf tournament that raises money towards Juvenile diabetes research. He donates $1,000 to KidSport Calgary for every goal he scores during the course of a season.

"My grandpa had the most influence on my hockey career and my mom tried to make as many games as she could. My dad came to a few but my grandpa always made sure that he came. I don't think he missed more than five of any baseball, hockey, or anything. What I really appreciated the most was, whether or not I had a bad game, and I knew I had bad games where I didn't try as hard as I could have, my parents, my grandpa, and grandma - they were always very positive. They never said you've got to work harder...what are you doing here? I appreciate that. They never criticized me. It's a game. Sometimes parents do take it a little too seriously. I think you want to keep it fun. Sure, we all want to win and take home trophies.It's awesome to win and I love winning...but keep it fun. Kids will work way harder if they're having fun.

"Looking back, I was fortunate to be able to go to some very good hockey schools. Howie Meeker came to town once with his hockey school. I went to the Sutter Tournament at Sylvan Lake when I was eight, nine years old.

"I never really got into fights at school except for maybe Grade Two when there were wrestling matches. I did get into a little bit of trouble. I gave the teachers a little bit of trouble like talking. I had a lot of energy. Today I'd probably be given a condition or something.

Back then I really did have a lot of energy...broke a lot of things around the house.

"I grew up with my mom. My dad was in Edmonton, but he was still pretty close. They were divorced when I was about one, and I was still close to my dad. I talked to him all the time. As far as I remember, they've been apart. I never knew them together, and I couldn't imagine them together. Their personalities are very different. They get along pretty well and that really helps to make things easier for me.

"I was very close to my grandparents too. I went to their place after school or they picked me up because my mom was working. I have siblings from my dad's new marriage, and I have two brothers and two sisters.

"Most of my friends were from hockey and baseball and the sports my mom got me involved in. It was difficult for my mom sometimes. You would go to these tournaments and everybody would be married. She was usually the only single one there. I think it was kind of hard talking to everyone as they had different things in common. But she came and I always wanted her there.

"We didn't have a lot of money because it was just my mom and a single income. We lived in a small apartment and it was good enough. We had everything we needed. My mom worked hard to make sure we weren't missing out on anything. Hockey and sports was pretty much all I did when I was younger. She always made sure I had top of the line equipment or as good equipment as other people. I didn't really think about the money. I think it was a lot harder on my mom. For me, she really did a good job. My grandparents were also there to help out. My mom really did most of it financially. From what I remember, she was always working.

"She always made time. Once a week and surely, once every two weeks, one day I'd get to bring a friend, and we'd go do something together that was some sort of an amusement thing. It meant a lot to me. It was our day and she'd always make sure, as busy as she was, she would take that time out and make sure it was our special time. She'd take me alone, but I'd always want to bring a friend."

Did he feel any prejudice growing up? *"I think Edmonton is a racially tolerant place. I didn't feel weird that my mom was white and I was black. There weren't too many issues. There was the odd thing, where you're fighting on the playground, but nothing really stands out where someone was really bullying me.*

Jarome and Friends

"I started hockey at age seven. My aunt got me into it. She took me down to the rink by my grandparents' home. I really loved it. My first couple of years were really slow because I was just learning to stand up. A few years into it, my grandpa made me aware of activities and got me into power skating and stuff to catch up. It was a local community power skating class, and the kids were pretty young teaching it. It wasn't always the most fun, but it helped me catch up. There were a lot of kids that started a lot earlier. In my first year, I was at the lowest I could start at. The second year I moved up slightly, then progressed.

"I was very fortunate (to have positive male role models). I look back, and I wouldn't change anything. I had the opportunity to be very close to my mom, dad, grandpa, and grandma. I was very fortunate to have them in my life. My grandparents definitely helped out a lot with their time, things like after school and making sure that dinner was there. It would have been a lot harder for my mom if she didn't have them there.

"I never had a problem passing in school. I didn't get unbelievable marks - probably around the 70s in elementary, maybe a little higher. Like other kids, you enjoy the things you do well, other things you just talk and stuff. I did all right. When I got to high school, my favorite subject was English. I really liked to come up with different ideas, essays, and writing. I thought maybe I'd be a lawyer because my dad is a lawyer. I loved debating and arguing when I was younger so I thought that might be a good fit. But I really always dreamed of being in the NHL."

Antawn Jamison

National Basketball Association Forward
www.antawnjamison.net

When the Charlotte Hornets moved to New Orleans, Antawn Jamison discovered the team would have to end its 13-year commitment of donating shoes each Christmas Eve to a homeless shelter. Jamison decided to purchase over $4,000 worth of shoes to keep the program running. He kicked off his "A Better Tomorrow" campaign December 2002 where residents of the Uptown Men's Shelter/George Shinn Center were fitted with new shoes. He also used the campaign as a way to provide hope for the less fortunate.

Jamison and former University of North Carolina teammate, Jerry Stackhouse, have purchased turkeys for the UNC Men's Basketball Team to distribute to local charities. He has served Thanksgiving dinners to residents of domestic violence shelters in the Bay Area through the Warriors annual Thanksgiving H.O.O.P. Caravan.

He purchased Golden State Warrior tickets for "Antawn's Army" for distribution to numerous youth organizations and students every month and hosted the team's annual Community Holiday Party at the Oakland Zoo, attended by 150 children from local youth centers.

Jamison started The Extra Effort Awards in 2003 for students in the Charlotte-Mecklenburg community. It's a program that rewards students (about 200) for their dedication and hard work. Some of the rewards include pizza parties, autographed certificates, and recognition on his website. The first annual Antawn C. Jamison Scholarship was presented in 2003 to two students from his former high school, Providence High. Students received a $4,000 ($1,000 for each year enrolled in college) scholarship if they have a good academic standing and display great citizenship at all times.

Joe Juneau

National Hockey League Center

It's not something you would expect from an NHL hockey player or any athlete, for that matter. Joe Juneau, with a bachelor degree in aeronautical engineering, is seeking a master degree in business. Not only that, Juneau plays in a rock band. A drummer for Offwings, the band performs at charity benefits. Proceeds from the sale of their compact discs go towards the Children's Hospital in Washington, D.C., Cam Neely Foundation, and the Cam Neely House (providing aid to families undergoing cancer treatment in the New England area).

"It was different for me growing up. There are more cars nowadays. The streets are busier. In my time, you could leave your nets on the street to play hockey. These days, you couldn't do that. Back then we had snow for the whole winter. Just the main road had salt or sand. Today all the roads are getting salted down so you're lucky if you can get a couple of days with a nice snow

surface to play street hockey. In my dad's era, it was more the outside rink. Evolution makes it different.

"For kids going to public schools in cities, maybe it's tougher for them. I'm not sure. My kids are too young and I'm not at that stage to be able to comment on that. When I grew up, at 10, 11, and 12 years old, we had kids smoking already and probably some kids starting drugs at 12 years old. I'm sure its still there today.

"I guess I can say I always had a good level of confidence in myself. Sometimes, in school, some of the stuff we studied, I kind of looked at it like we were forced to study. Whatever came easy to me, I never worked at it, except for doing my problems and homework. I listened a little bit in class and waited for the test. The classes where you had more problems, where it wasn't as natural, then maybe I was forced to work at it a bit more. When you get good grades, it helps build you up. If you don't have good grades, in my case, a lot of times, it was because I never studied."

How would life be different had he not been involved in sports? *"I would say different. Growing up, getting taught to work as a team, to achieve a goal...I always played other sports, like swimming, cross country, running, and skiing. I can relate to sport both individually and as a team. I think it's very important. It's very special to win a tournament, being part of a hockey team, handball, or basketball. Kids have to come together and work for the same goals. Later on in life, if they've got a job in a big company and they have to work on a project, research, or whatever, they know what its about. I would not be the same if I went through my life without being part of teams like that.*

"Besides my parents, coaches, and they were a big part of it, I worked with one of my uncles in construction during the summer. It was kind of like a first job. My uncle was the owner of the company. I looked up to him and was learning to work, learning to make money, and make a living.

"I think it's important to think about the first day you make it into the NHL and even before that. In my case, I remember when I was in college. I ended up being well known in the area around my university. I think at that time it was important for me to start making sure I was not doing stupid things...things that could end up in the paper. For me, it happened before the NHL, when I was about 19 or 20.

"You've got to be smart about it. You obviously want to have fun. Life is too short. There's no way you can sit home and do nothing because you don't want to show a bad example. There are a lot of chances to have fun, go over the edge, and do crazy things, but you've got to make sure that those things are not stupid things and that you're doing them for the right reasons...to have fun and not to hurt anybody."

Paul Kariya

National Hockey League Left Wing

Just ask the Children's Hospital of Orange County about Paul Kariya and his commitment to the community. Besides serving as the hospital's All-Star Kids Captain, he donates significant dollars to it as well. His substantial involvement with children's charities earned him the NHL's 2002 MAC Award. He is also the national spokesman for Hockey Canada's Initiation Program - a campaign that focuses on teaching skills first in minor hockey.

"It's important to give back to where I came from. Obviously, I wouldn't be where I was today if I didn't have hockey in my life and all the great coaches and programs I was lucky enough to be a part of growing up. I was basically able to go through all the programs - Under 16, Under 17, and the Olympics."

Regarding the controversy over nine year olds body checking in hockey: *"Obviously there's an age you have to put it in. You don't want to put kids in too early and maybe lose some that don't like it at that age. At the same time, it is important to have it because it is a part of the game. You do have to learn how to take a hit and give a hit. Not too young, but the younger you start, when a kid's not fully developed, you're not going to do as much damage. They're more pliable. They can learn the right way early."*

On funding, volunteers, and improvement: *"Hockey's a very expensive sport to play and I think that's the only drawback. You probably lose a lot of great hockey players. You look at basketball or even soccer. You just need to buy a pair of cleats or hightops, and go out and play. In hockey, there's a lot of equipment. I don't have an answer on how to solve the funding issue, but obviously, when players that have made it give back either financially or through programs, it helps a lot.*

"In general, our whole society doesn't give enough to the people that need it. When you talk about (corporate philanthropy), you can always say well, there are probably people that need it more than kids that want to play hockey...people who don't have enough food on the table or live in a proper house. It's a touchy subject."

Why is it so important to keep amateur sports programs going? *"Because they make you a better person in the long run. That's the bottom line. Kids that participate in sports are a lot less likely to get into trouble after school. They understand the importance of being a team player and being a part of a bigger unit. That's what society is. You're not an individual out there. You're part of a bigger group. Just being a part of sports, whether you compete in them or not, is important."*

On the role model status: *"It's a no-brainer. When you've been given a lot in your life, it's a no-brainer. You want to give back. I've always been very fortunate growing up and having great coaches and great programs. I wouldn't be in the NHL without those programs."*

96

Kariya spent two years at University of Maine and was the first freshman to ever win the Hobey Baker award for the top U.S. college player. He won the Hockey East Rookie of the Year and Player of the Year in the same year (1993). *"I didn't know if I was going to make it (to the NHL) so getting an education was really important to me. It's important to have a balance in your life.*

"We had five kids in the family and we're all very close. Anytime you want to play hockey or any other games, there was always a brother or sister around to play with. It was a great feeling to have that support around you. Every hockey parent knows how much it takes. One of my parents was always at my games or practices. It was really nice to have them at whatever I was doing.

"Road hockey, shooting pucks in the backyard...I did other sports too. Hockey wasn't my life. I did everything."

Jason Kidd

National Basketball Association Guard
Jason Kidd Foundation

The Jason Kidd Foundation was launched in 1999 to improve the welfare of youth. The foundation provides funds for children's medical research and gives to organizations advocating the needs and interests of children. Opportunity Project, The Christopher Reeve Paralysis Foundation, The Marty Lyons Foundation, the Starlight Foundation, and the Upward Foundation are among those that Kidd supports.

Joumana Kidd accompanied 25 children from the Newark Salvation Army on a Christmas shopping spree for toys with a "salary cap" from her husband's foundation. Jason Kidd played Secret Santa to a needy child's family and spent the day opening gifts, treated them to dinner, and played a game of basketball. The Kidd family also joined the annual holiday party of the Boys and Girls Clubs of Newark and sang Christmas carols with the children.

The prestigious Thurman Munson Award from the Association for the Help of Retarded Children recognized Kidd for his foundation's efforts in helping the community.

A member of the NBA All-Star Reading Team and the Nets All-Star Reading Team, Kidd was named to the Newark Star Ledger's Signs of Freedom literacy support team. He plays an active role talking to kids about the importance of reading and education through reading events and public service announcements.

Ian Laperriere
National Hockey League Center

His teammates voted him the "Most Inspirational Player" and the Los Angeles Kings Booster Club named him the "Most Popular Player" in 2000-2001. He received the same honor in 1996-1997. Ian Laperriere is truly one of the NHL nice guys. His favorite charity is Big Brother and Big Sister of America.

"My main thing is just to be a good person. On the ice, we don't always look like a good person. I just try to be the best person I can be in life, not only in hockey, but outside the rink. I think that's the way I can give a good example. I'm in the NHL. I made it. Some guys might go in and change and be a different person. I try not to change. I try to stick with the way my parent's raised me.

"Every summer, I have a golf tournament and every year, there's a young kid who might have some disease. Every time I see that it makes me feel lucky - thankful for what I do. When I see those young girls and boys, they'll never have a life like me. By doing the golf tournament, I just try to help them have an easier life, but I know they won't. My teammates are like that too. We feel pretty lucky.

"My parents were my role models. They raised me as a good kid. By what I'm doing, I try to lead by example. That's the way my parents were. (If I didn't have hockey) probably, because of my parents, I'd be in school and have something to sit back on. I always wanted to be a policeman. I think I might have been one right now if it wasn't for hockey.

"All the discipline you have to go through, if you want to do okay the next season, you have to work out. All those little things you can take into life. If you want something, you have to sacrifice other things if you want to reach your goal. I think that's what hockey brought to me. The focus. I have to focus so much on my goal that I have to sacrifice. That's pretty much life."

On the camaraderie: *"It's just like a big family, I guess. That's the thing I'm going to miss the most when I retire. I'll miss the game, big time, but I'll miss being around the guys. You just can't describe that. People outside won't talk the way we talk to each other in the locker room. Sometimes, what a colleague might say, if I were to tell that to a friend back home, or anybody... You just can't describe it. I just try to enjoy every moment. It's a short career."*

Misconceptions on players: *"Any kind of job in the world, you'll find that some people are not as nice. It doesn't matter how much money you get. Ask any real fan what kind of people hockey players are. Too many people rip up players saying they're cocky. They never stop to sign autographs. Most of us will. Like I said, there are bad people in any kind of job and there are some in hockey. That's the thing with hockey players. We realize we're lucky to do what we're doing. To say we're cocky about it, I don't see it. But I know there are a couple guys out there who are like that."*

George Lynch

National Basketball Association Forward

"George's Gang", soon to be called, "George's Hustle Bunch," is a program where George Lynch purchases 20 season tickets to donate back to kids. Some of the recipients have been the Fearless Tigers Cultural Arts Center, a martial arts program; "Faith House," a youth services program dealing with lifestyle counseling and designed to help kids with math and sciences; and an East New Orleans group called "Stanka," which provides math \ encouragement and support services.

Lynch champions many programs for kids: the Boys Scouts of New Orleans, Stanka Tutorial and Martial Arts Program, and Boys to Men Mentoring Program. He visits several charity functions and is a Read to Achieve All-Star. Lynch has also purchased and delivered 300 turkeys to Charlotte agencies and residents.

He was named the NBA's Hometown Hero of the Month of February 2001.

Karl Malone

National Basketball Association Forward
The Karl Malone Foundation for Kids

Karl Malone is a man who needs no fanfare. In fact, he prefers to keep his charity work out of the spotlight. Perhaps it's to let his philanthropic recipients keep their privacy. Whatever the reason, Malone has made an enormous difference throughout his career.

The Karl Malone Foundation for Kids helps youth and their families with financial assistance. That includes paying their bills. He has donated $200,000 worth of supplies to Navajo Indians, paid off a mortgage for a family with four sick children, paid for a playground at a local elementary school for the handicapped, and bought vans for special-needs families.

Malone personally handed out clothing for a coat drive his foundation sponsored for a homeless shelter. He has invited Make-A-Wish children to his home and has been actively involved in the Utah Special Olympics.

Malone received the 1998 Henry B. Iba Award for athletes who go out of their way to help others.

Shawn Marion

National Basketball Association Forward

When Shawn Marion signed his NBA contract, he donated one million dollars to charity. It was his way of saying thanks for the opportunities he received as a young man growing up in a poor neighborhood outside of Chicago.

Basketball steered him in the right direction. Instead of taking to the street, he chose to frequent a 24-hour gym, hitting the court with friends until two or three in the morning. He noticed that same opportunity wasn't offered in other neighborhoods, which is why he decided to fund a 24-hour facility in Phoenix. Scholarships will be offered to kids who can't afford to shoot hoops.

In the process of starting a foundation in Chicago, Marion tends to focus on three types of charities: cancer victims and their families, children's basketball leagues, and organizations that help people become first time home owners.

He participates in Read to Achieve rallies, hospital visits, basketball clinics, and Marion helped fund a reading room at Glendale's Stewart Branch of the Boys and Girls Club.

The 2001-2002 Division NBA Sportsmanship Award was presented to Marion for being a player who best represents the ideals of sportsmanship on the court.

Donyell Marshall

National Basketball Association Forward
The Donyell Marshall Foundation www.givingback.org

The City of Chicago has benefited greatly from the presence of Donyell Marshall. Besides guiding the Bulls' community relations' efforts, he has volunteered his time, and provided financial contributions to many organizations throughout the area.

The Giving Back Fund is a national nonprofit organization helping professional athletes and entertainers establish and maintain charitable foundations for philanthropic giving. It provides these groups with strategic and legal consultation, financial and day-to-day planning, grant making, public relations, administrative support, website development and management, and special event coordination.

The Donyell Marshall Foundation is a member of The Giving Back Fund and advocates organizations that provide youth with experiences they might not otherwise have. Trips to cultural institutions, athletic and entertainment events, athletic and outdoor recreation programs - these are adventures the foundation supports. Each year, the Donyell Marshall Celebrity Golf Tournament helps raise money for the foundation.

"Donyell's Deputies" is a 25-seat children's charity section that Marshall personally greets before each home game. He has invited members of his Deputy group to attend games in Philadelphia when the Bulls traveled there for road trips.

Marshall provided $100 gift cards and led a shopping spree for 30 children from Chicago's Martin Luther King Boys and Girls Club.

Fitted with a chair of his own, he played in a full wheelchair basketball game with patients from the Shriners Hospitals for Children after presenting them with a $10,000 donation from the team. At another team function, he made the largest purchase at a Holiday Heroes fundraiser.

Marshall hosts an annual basketball camp and is actively involved in the Read to Achieve program.

Tracy McGrady

National Basketball Association Guard
The Tracy McGrady Foundation www.t-mac.com

Iran Brown's life was turned upside down when he became the victim of a D.C. sniper. The NBA fan's plight caught the attention of Tracy McGrady, who delivered a taped message and autographed items to his hospital bed. But the kindness didn't end there. McGrady treated Brown's entire family to a vacation in Orlando, which included tickets to see the Magic play and personal time with the NBA star.

At the 2003 NBA All-Star Weekend in Atlanta, thanks to McGrady, the Miller family (Melissa and her eight-year old daughter Tessa) was in attendance. Charles Miller (husband and father), a member of the Florida National Guard, was away serving with the military in Ft. Stewart, Georgia as he prepared to head overseas. McGrady took time out for Melissa and Tessa during the weekend's festivities. It was a small gesture of appreciation for the sacrifice U.S. servicemen and women face each and every day.

McGrady has spent time hosting four different Make-A-Wish children and their families at an NBA game and is active with the Read to Achieve program. He has been the Magic's spokesperson for the Fly Away program - an essay contest within the local Boys and Girls Clubs, where two winners get to travel with the team to two different cities.

The Tracy McGrady Foundation was created to help "kids at risk" in the Orlando area. It focuses on helping young people realize their full potential as they develop into responsible, productive citizens. McGrady also works with other players' foundations, such as Darrell Armstrong's Celebrity Weekend (raising money for premature babies) and Mike Miller's Bowl-A-Thon (benefiting Second Harvest Food Bank and Coalition for the Homeless).

Mark McLoughlin

Canadian Football League Kicker
Stay In School www.stampeders.com

He was nominated in 1994 and twice named as the Canadian Football League's Man of the Year, winning the Tom Pate Memorial Award in 1997 and 1995. While considered a clutch performer when the game gets tight on the field, Mark McLoughlin's off-field accomplishments are what he is most proud of. He started the "Stay In School" program in 1992. He recently hung up his cleats to assume the role of President of the Calgary Stampeders.

"I grew up in Liverpool, England. My family moved to Canada when I was ten years old. The area we grew up in was pretty rough. You really had to develop your street smarts and make sure you covered all your angles. You really had to build your thick skin and be sort of a tough kid.

"The one thing that has always been a positive for me is that my family environment was very, very supportive. They let me make my own choices, whether they felt they were right or wrong. Through that, they also let me experience those bad experiences as part of learning but were always there for me to lean upon when I ran into some tough times.

"My family came to Canada because, at that time, the economy in England was going downhill. They were looking at a future life for

my sister and me. We moved to Winnipeg in 1976, where I went to one year of elementary school, junior high, and high school. It was through that whole process of being challenged with education, not so much that I couldn't accomplish the task or that I was not smart enough, I started choosing a path that was taking me in the wrong direction.

"Through those challenges, an individual helped guide me on the right path, which opened many doors for me. It enabled me to go onto the University of South Dakota, play football, and do what I'm presently doing today.

"The assistant principal of the high school I attended in Winnipeg was also, at one time, a soccer coach. That relationship was somewhat of a fatherly figure. For him to take time out and apply it directly to me, focus on me and me only, I thought that was very valuable. When I look at people today in our community - senior executives, chief executive officers, managers, or frontline people, it really doesn't matter...if they're willing to take the time to lend a hand to youth, to help guide and direct, and at the same time share some of their own personal challenges, we create a bit of a game plan for them.

"When I look back at why I'm totally committed to supporting education as being the foundation for life, it's because of my own experiences. We find that a lot of kids today are challenged. There are so many things for them to do, to take away their attention and focus of what's important. They go for the instant gratification rather than a long-term plan for their life. With those challenges and influences, I think it's important for us, as a community in general, to be there, be supportive, and redirect them.

"A lot of organizations that have mentoring programs in place are vital because a lot of our young people today are not comfortable in addressing big issues with their parents or with other family members. They're more open to addressing issues with people

they've come into contact with in a mentoring environment. A lot of our youth have their arms wide open, willing to embrace them. As a community, we need to fulfill that embracement. We also need to allow them to understand where they can look for help.

"I'm very involved with a lot of charities. I've had a commitment to the Multiple Sclerosis Society for a number of years. I'm involved in a lot of youth organizations. One of the things very close to me is my "Stay-In-School" program. I do well over 100 school visits per year throughout all of Southern Alberta. It's a broad demographic of students. I talk to them about the importance of what education can provide to them in the future... the whole foundation aspect.

"Every young person today has some kind of dream or goal they would like to achieve. A lot of them don't know how to go about it. A lot of them don't have the self-confidence that we do. Sometimes they get a little despondent in not getting the support. As a community, it's important that we continue our efforts to allow our young people to know that, outside of the classroom, the doors are open. There are people in the community who do care about them and are willing to give them their time to share some of their experiences, to hopefully allow them to fulfill some of their dreams.

"I get inspired all the time by the kids. I think kids today are pretty unique. They're a lot brighter than I think we give them credit for. They're a lot smarter than we probably were at their age. At the same time, they do have a lot of challenges. The thing that does inspire me is the fact that 100 percent of the kids I speak to in schools are in school. To me that's inspiring because they are committed to bettering themselves. Whether it's a complete focus on education or a combination of education and athletics, whatever it is, as long as they're learning every day. We always hear the analogy that education is a journey. It's not a specific destination. That's so true in today's workplace. The more we can

encourage complete learning, not just academically, complete learning for the whole person, it's important.

"I've spoke to kids at an elementary level that have come up to me after I've spoken at a grade 12 graduation, where I've been part of that whole process. For me, I get a chance to graduate with them. I also have a lot of friends with kids in the school system and get that recognition back that what I had to say had some impact. All I'm hoping for is for one individual to experience what I experienced by having somebody assist and help guide them.

"To be able to do what I've done for the past 16 years is truly a dream come true. Without that guidance and support and the educational foundation, there is no way I'd be doing what I'm doing. I dread to think of what the options would be if I hadn't gone completed high school or university.

"Some of the guys I grew up with are doing the same sort of work - labor-type jobs we did when we were in high school. Even though I left a job that was well paying at that time to focus on education, the investment is a thousand times better than it would have been if I hadn't done that. Sometimes our young people are inspired by money. What they're earning today isn't going to be enough for them to live on in the future. They're just not aware of how important the whole financial picture is and what education can do."

How important is it for an athlete to send the message? "I believe they do listen more. Whether I disagree with that...it's a reality. As athletes, we need to understand that and conduct ourselves as such. At the end of the day, we have a choice of whether we want to be an athlete and have a community profile or whether we don't. If we're not comfortable with that, we should probably get out of the business because that does come with the territory. It's part of our role and responsibility. As I look at it from a Canadian Football League standpoint, it's important to give back to the *community. As a league, we're gate-driven. If individuals do not come and buy tickets to support us as a team or as a league, then we don't exist. The opportunity we have, as athletes, wouldn't exist. It's not like there are ample football leagues out there, where 100 percent of all CFL football players can go and play in some other league. In a way, what I give back to the community, what I'm doing is saying, I appreciate the opportunity I have as an athlete. I appreciate the support of our fans, the community in general. This is just something small that I can give back in return, whether it's a financial contribution, my time, or whether it's my experience.*

"I have been involved in an amateur organization and a professional organization, seeking support and sponsorship through direct contributions. My answer to a lot of companies, that want to just focus primarily on the professional side of things because of the exposure, if there isn't an investment on the amateur component of athletics, the professional side doesn't happen. The overall development, the type of individual required to succeed at a professional level goes beyond ability. There are more expectations on how they conduct themselves in public, public speaking, investing back into the community, working with corporate sponsors...it goes beyond the field or the rink. The demand of the corporate sector is changing. If the investment happens at a very young age at the grassroots level, all of a sudden, you're helping to cultivate that change, that philosophy in the individual. The investment is ultimately going to pay off down the road. Whether it's kids age four, five, or six playing soccer, on the rink, or student athletes at the college level, that's where our focus has to be as a community. The types of individuals that we're creating - a very small percentage, become professional athletes. The larger percentage become good solid citizens. The investment is not just from a sporting standpoint. You're investing in the person and on the impact of the community as a whole.

"I think a city handcuffs itself in some respects. It promotes the fact that it's a solid community of volunteers. All of a sudden, it

becomes an expectation that anything you want done is going to be done by volunteers. The demand that's put on individuals' time from a working and home environment really cuts down what they can apply towards volunteering. It's not that people don't want to do it. It's just the reality of life. The expectations are, if you don't have volunteers, then things don't exist. What is the return on investment from the volunteer standpoint? What are they giving and what do they get out of it? From a corporate standpoint...what are they giving and what do they get out of it? It may not happen immediately. The more we can do at the grassroots level, the more we can encourage people to participate.

"In particularly with soccer, what you're finding is a lot of club systems are hiring fairly well paid technical directors. Because the parents, who have these kids in the club systems, are paying a fair amount of money to participate, they want to know what they're getting out of it. It's important for professional teams to engage themselves back to the community by putting on clinics, engaging the professional players, management, and staff to assist people to get coaching and training, to allow them to make sure, from a technical standpoint, that what they have to offer is valuable. It certainly does not take away from the individual who gives of their time. There is still a role because nobody else will do it. But you have to make it worthwhile for kids. You have to make it valuable. Technically, the games move at such a quick pace and the development happens so fast, if they're technically not sound, there are a lot of things that can happen. Injuries, whether it's a continual negative experience that forces the player to not want to participate, it takes that whole fun and enjoyment aspect out of the game and it can hinder kids for their lifetime. It's important we have the right people. It's also important that the professional teams and players give up their own experience to assist these people who are doing this on a volunteer basis."

Would you agree that how a person plays the game of sport is how they play the game of life? "To me, the game of sport is a component of my life. It's no bigger or important than any other aspect of it. First and foremost is my family. From there, it's a part of what I do. It's not the be all, end all. I've always wanted to use it as something to be able to leverage me to do other things... community work, my work with kids. It's a platform. I never want to be defined as just a football guy because I think I can offer more than that.

"My work ethic is just as strong towards football as it is to my family as it is to my business and everything else I do. I also understand I'm going to fail on the football field. I'm going to fail off the football field. Failure is a part of being successful. In order to be successful, you have to understand how to fail. You have to understand when you do fail, it's teaching you how to succeed those experiences. If I'm lucky, 20 percent of the time, I'm going to be unsuccessful on the football field. If I am successful 80 percent of the time, I'm probably an all-star. If I can say 20 percent of my life, I'm probably going to fail, 80 percent I'll be successful, I'll probably take those odds too. My commitment is from a training standpoint, from a mental visonary standpoint, commitment to my teammates and everything else is as strong as what I do off the field.

"Football is the type of sport where, emotionally and physically, everybody on that team has to exert everything. Everything is left out there. When you're not successful, it just makes it that much harder to accept. Especially in playoffs. The unfortunate thing about football is that it's a one game shot. They're not round robins or best of seven. Regardless of past performances or anything else, it all comes down to everybody executing at the highest level on that particular day. There are some great teams, and I've been a part of them, where that hasn't happened. We've had great regular season records - 15-3, 14-4, and might even have been 16-2, where we haven't succeeded in the playoffs. It's just because on that one day, that one game, everybody wasn't working up to par.

"You have to have solid alumni foundations. When you're playing, you spend probably more time within a team environment - you're individual teammates, than you do with your own family. That locker room becomes a second home to you. You fully engage yourself. You leave your emotions wide open on the table. Everybody gets a chance to see that. That family, once it starts to break up, it does have a huge emotional attachment. For some players, it's very difficult to get over. Some have a very hard time making the transition from the sporting world to the real-life working world. You hear about people, whether it's from suicides, financial collapses, or nervous breakdowns - they're never able to get through that transition. It's no different than some kind of divorce, home breakup, where it takes a long time emotionally to get over it. You're open - wide open. Your hearts are open for everybody to pick at because they are part of your family.

"You always hear stories how the team sport environment enabled individuals to overcome many challenges. It was the team sport that pulled them through. It was the team that kept them in school. Outside of that, they really didn't have anything else. It is important what it creates for later in life. As long as you understand what you have to do individually in order to succeed, it also helps you understand the role you have to play within the team environment for the entire team to succeed. It's no different than the working world. If you're an entrepreneur, you're still accountable for other people or you're expecting other people to assist in some areas. Within a large corporation, you're particular task is something you have to excel at but you're part of a bigger picture."

Gary Payton

National Basketball Association Guard
The Gary Payton Foundation www.gpfoundation.org

Gary Payton turned Treshawn "Tre" Mathis's world of
hopelessness and pain into a world of hope and laughter. The two
met in Seattle, when Payton participated in a toy give-away with
the Ronald McDonald House. With his lymphoma in remission,
Tre's parents believed the good news stemmed from a combination
of chemotherapy treatments and meeting Gary Payton. "The
Glove" put a smile on the young man's face and gave him a
newfound interest in watching basketball.

The Ronald McDonald House is one of the charities favored by
The Gary Payton Foundation. The foundation helps organizations
and events that build opportunities for at-risk youth residing in the
greater regions of Seattle, Washington, and Oakland, California, in
the areas of education, recreation, and overall wellness.

It was a way to help ease the burden of families of cancer patients
who were unable to spend Christmas at home. "How 'The Glove'
Gave Christmas" was launched in December 2002, where 50
children from the Ronald McDonald House were bused with their
families to the FAO Schwarz store in downtown Seattle. Payton's
foundation presented each child a $100 shopping spree.

"How 'The Glove' Gave Christmas" also treated a young
Somalia-born boy to the experience of a lifetime. Housed in a
Kenyan refugee camp with his mother and three siblings prior to
his arrival to the United States, Yasin Abdullahi spent a few days
with Payton after his school nominated him as a model student. A
limousine ride to an NBA game was only the beginning. Yasin took
his post at courtside as a ball boy, and then accompanied Payton's
team on a road trip to Portland. He paid visit to Beaverton's Nike
campus and left with a truckload of Payton gear. He worked as a
ball boy again before returning home to his family.

Four hundred families in Washington's Snohomish County have felt the pinch of declining resources. Gary Payton and the Gary Payton Foundation helped brighten the holiday by donating a complete Thanksgiving dinner to ensure each family didn't have to go hungry.

Payton penned "Confidence Counts", an autobiographical children's book published in 1999. His charity basketball game raises money for Big Brothers of King County.

Jalen Rose

National Basketball Association Guard/Forward
Jalen Rose Foundation www.jalenrosefoundation.org

When a player is traded, his philanthropic efforts generally won't end at the last port. Such is the case with Jalen Rose. A trade from Indiana to Chicago only allowed him an opportunity to expand his foundation into his new community.

The Jalen Rose Chicago Children's Foundation, part of the Giving Back Fund, was inspired by the tragedy at Chicago's second-story E2 nightclub in February 2003. Initiated by a fight between two women, guards used pepper spray in an attempt to control the crowd, causing a stampede towards a locked stairway exit. The crush killed 21 nightclub patrons and injured 50. Rose set up the foundation as a way to provide children, who have experienced the death of a parent, with essential needs. His initial contribution to the fund was $25,000.

The Jalen Rose Foundation also invests in programs that support single parent families. It works with community kitchens, providing meals for individuals and families in need and helps nonprofit organizations assisting children with their primary education and/or college goals. The foundation's grants are distributed in Detroit, Chicago, and Indianapolis.

Rose volunteers and adds a personal touch to every financial contribution he makes. Demonstrating his sincere commitment to making a difference in people's lives, he meets with people he champions. At Chicago's Lawrence Hall Youth Services, personally doled out parcels, which included athletic wear, gym shoes, $100 gift cards, and toys, to abused and neglected children.

He's involved in Chicago Mayor Richard Daley's Council on Fitness - an activity awareness initiative that encourages Chicagoans to get involved in physical recreation, sports, and active lifestyles.

"The Rose Garden" provides tickets to 20 single-parent or at-risk children to attend each Bulls home game. He personally meets with each child, gives them a t-shirt, and poses for a group photo. For each assist, he donates $50 to Boys and Girls Clubs in Chicago.

He co-hosted an NBA All-Star Game at the United Center and delivered 1,000 tickets to students neighboring schools prior to tip off. He is an active member of the NBA Read to Achieve program, organized a summer charity comedy show, and purchased tickets for needy children to attend the first-time CharitaBulls fundraiser.

Rose received the Fox Sports Net Chicago's 2003 Bull of the Year Award and donated $5,000 to the March of Dimes.

Bryon Russell

National Basketball Association Forward
The Bryon Russell Foundation

Since 1999, The Byron Russell Foundation has contributed to Toys for Tots, Rape Recovery Center (Utah), Make-a-Wish Foundation, Adoption Exchange of Utah, Ogden Youth Authority (Utah), Boys and Girls Club of Murray (Utah), and St. Vincent de Paul (homeless shelter in Utah).

For the past three years, the foundation has organized an annual charity event to raise money; the first two years a celebrity softball game and the third year a celebrity basketball game to name a few.

With his wife, Kimberli, the Russells are committed to promoting positive change. The couple has sponsored a family for the Wizards Family-to-Family Holiday gift giveaway by purchasing clothes, toys, and food. Russell purchases items for Thanksgiving gift baskets with some of his teammates. He and Kim also served a Thanksgiving lunch to 100 seniors.

Russell operates basketball camps for underprivileged children.

Brian Shaw

National Basketball Association Guard
The Brian Shaw Foundation

Brian Shaw lost his parents and only sister in a fatal car accident. Through the mourning process, he established The Brian Shaw Foundation in 1995, to instill some of the life lessons his parents taught him to others. The foundation stresses the importance of parent/child development and parent/child involvement.

The foundation initiated "The Brian Shaw NBA Basketball Camp" in Oakland, where kids are taught, encouraged, and challenged to strive at everything they do both on and off the court. Shaw contributes to the Barbara E. Shaw Scholarship Fund, which annually affords two African-American women the opportunity to attend the National Black Child Development Institute Conference.

The "Just Say Thanks By Giving" Thanksgiving Dinner was co-founded in 1993 by Shaw and fellow Oakland native, Gary Payton. It provides a complete Thanksgiving meal to Oakland families that are trying to make "ends meet". Approximately 1,100 families were served in 2002. Over 12,100 families have been fed since the program began. The two NBA stars have enlisted fellow players, local dignitaries, community members, and local businesses to help shed Thanksgiving cheer.

Shaw hosts the Brian Shaw Celebrity Pool Tournament at Universal Studios in Orlando and an annual bass-fishing tournament benefiting Parent-Child Development Centers, Inc. of Oakland and Orlando. He also joined fellow Lakers for a youth fishing program for inner-city youth.

Eric Snow

National Basketball Association Guard
The Twenty Foundation
Eric's Challenge (see www.sixers.com)

Eric Snow takes fatherhood very seriously. He makes an ongoing commitment to stress the importance of fatherhood and shares the spotlight with his sons. He does this through the Father-Son One-on-One Program.

An initiative of the One-on-One Program is the On the Court Program, which can be accessed through the Sixers website and Eric's Challenge. Snow sponsors a contest for a father-son duo to win Sixers tickets. Snow greets each winner, introduces them to his teammates prior to the game, and each father-son duo is recognized both at the game and on the Sixers website.

In the Community Program is also part of One-on-One. Outings with Snow and his son are auctioned off to another father-son duo to raise money for Sixers charities. In 2002, Andy and Russ Smale accompanied the Snows in a super box at a National Football League game.

Snow hosts an exclusive basketball clinic for 60 New Jersey father-son duos as part of a grassroots community initiative called the Fathers Go Get Your Sons Program. Fathers and sons join Snow and his son on the court and learn to develop the fundamental skills of basketball. Snow holds a question and answer period at the clinic's conclusion and shares his own experiences with fatherhood and on being an NBA player.

"I didn't necessarily start and commit to these initiatives for any personal recognition," claims Snow. *"I wanted people to know that there were some good fathers in the NBA. This program is for fathers in general. But in the NBA, many fathers were getting a bad rap. There are far more good fathers than there were fathers who perhaps were not living up to their responsibilities. Just like in the general public...there are many more good fathers. I just wanted to do something to recognize and encourage those good father. Above everything else, I love spending time with my three boys E.J., Darius and Jarren."*

Snow donates $20 per steal and $10 per assists to Steals and Assists Donation Program, which raises money for charity.

Jerry Stackhouse

National Basketball Association Forward
Triple Threat Foundation www.jerrystackhouse.com

Jerry Stackhouse has a bachelor's degree in African American Studies and became the youngest American to serve on the board of a major hospital system when named as a Board of Trustee for the Rehabilitation Institute of Michigan.

His "More to Life" campaign implements projects designed to assist the less fortunate during the holidays. It's name is Stackhouse's way of showing others that he knows there is more to life than wealth - that caring for the community is important...such as providing dinners to over 100 people at Thanksgiving.

After losing two sisters to diabetes and with both parents suffering from Type 2 diabetes, Stackhouse organized The Triple Threat Fund to help others burdened from the same disease. He hopes to ensure funds are available for the education, prevention, and treatment of diabetes and for research of African American and Hispanic populations. He also addresses the issues of obesity and lack of exercise in youth, offering ideas and resources to encourage a healthy lifestyle.

Stackhouse spoke on Capitol Hill September 2001, accompanied by Colorado Democrat, Diana DeGette, and Washington State Republican, George Nethercutt, both members of the American Diabetes Association and co-chairs of the Congressional Diabetes Congress. He stressed there wasn't enough education on the prevention and treatment of diabetes and suggested policymakers should provide more funding and focus on this issue.

Jamie Storr

National Hockey League Goaltender

He was the Los Angeles Kings' first round pick in the 1994 NHL Entry Draft (chosen seventh overall). Jamie Storr has played backup to some of the league's best goalies and puckstopped for his hockey hero - Wayne Gretzky. His summer hockey school calls for celebrating pride in one's heritage.

"I'm trying to defeat racism in sports and the general community. It's impossible to do, but role models on professional teams can definitely have an affect on a community in a positive manner. It's something I take very seriously.

"I'm half Japanese. It's important for athletes, especially in high-end sports, to take a serious approach in their own community. The Japanese community I feel a real strong bond with because of my heritage. It gives me an opportunity to work

with a lot of people who have no idea what hockey's all. It broadens the horizon, not only on the diversity issue, but also by giving them positive feedback on the sport of hockey. It's a part of NHL Diversity, but it's a separate program run through the LA Kings and myself. This isn't something that we have to do. I just have the privilege of going in and being the spokesperson. I don't have a lot of time during the year to focus on anything but the game so any time I have, it's already set up and ready to run, and I just step in and talk to a lot of people who I have a very special bond with.

"I never had that so that's why it's very important. I had the face, as does every other child growing up, of diversity throughout schools and the community. It's something that I approached as a professional athlete, to be the role model I never had. I never had a Japanese-Canadian person to look up to other than my mother. I was ashamed, when I was a kid, that I was half Japanese. That's probably one of the biggest letdowns I look back on. If I could change one thing it would be, not to look at what other people see you as...the color of your skin or your heritage. Instead, be proud to be unique and stand up for it. It's something I'm trying to teach these kids. When other people look at you a little different, stand up for yourself. Be proud of who you are. Paul Kariya's playing in the NHL. I'm playing in the NHL. Some of the best baseball players in the world are from Japan. Be proud of your heritage. Not because there are role models out there that are the same as you, but you could be one of those role models down the road. They can have something to look up to. They can say it's cool to be half Japanese instead of running away from it. Even if it helps one child to look at being proud of who he is, it's worthwhile for me to do it.

"As an adult, you're able to overcome any prejudice - not letting it affect you in a negative manner, realizing, I can choose the people I hang out with, the people I talk to. I choose to choose people who are a positive influence on me. I know there are negative *influences out there. The people you surround yourself with are the people you are most like. If you're successful, a hard worker, and positive, you're a positive influence, not only on yourself, your family, and your community, but mostly the people you hang around. If you're a negative influence, negative person, you're going to tend to hang out with that kind of crowd. There are a lot more actions you can take as an adult than there are as a child. I played with Nathan Lafayette, who was half African-American and half Irish. He said the hardest thing for him was, he wasn't accepted by the white community because he wasn't really white. He wasn't accepted by the black community because he wasn't really black. There wasn't a community for him. I think it's important for those people, especially as role models, to step up and be a positive influence. There are a lot of kids out there like them. Stepping out to talk about it or talk to the community that they feel positive about it...it has a big effect.*

"I do this because I get enjoyment out of it, not because I have to. My mother passed away eight years ago and the only Japanese trace I feel is through her. Now that she's passed away, I feel even stronger about reaching out to that community. Every time I'm able to talk to those people, it's from the heart. It has a meaning.

"My brother is a teacher back home in Ontario. Sometimes he has good classes. Sometimes he has bad classes. It's tough when you have kids that don't want to listen or learn. I said, even if you can get one child in class and make a difference in his life, you don't have to make a difference in 29 children's lives. So when I do the diversity training, if one person picks it up, it's worthwhile. It makes me feel even closer to my heritage. That's important for me. Hockey's just a game. We've got the luxury of making a lot of money. There are a lot more things out there that are important in life. To be a positive person, the community is a lot more important.

"People listen to sports athletes and people with a little bit of power behind them a lot more than they listen to the average person walking on the street. I think it's, not only opportunity for an

athlete, but it's something you have to do for the influence on young children today. Those are the next great people in the world. My child will have a role model to look up to when he gets older.

"I had a little girl, the first time I ran the diversity clinic, who was half Japanese and half American. She came up to me and said, "Hey, Jamie, I'm just like you." I asked what she meant by that. She said, "I'm Japanese. I'm just like you." She felt important because of that. That's what it's all about. It's just realizing it's not the color of their skin. It's not their heritage or what they're going to become in the future. It's what's inside of them. It doesn't matter if you're black, white, Asian - any type of race. They can succeed in life if they sacrifice and work hard. You realize if children can put those excuses aside, instead of saying, "Well, I didn't get a fair chance because I'm Asian," then they realize it's up to them. So then they can look themselves in the mirror and be proud of who they are and work towards goals they feel are achievable and cut the crap aside. Don't feel sorry because they were born into this world under their heritage. We're trying to make them realize, when they're born into this world, they're given an opportunity to do something in life and if they take a positive aspect to it, work hard and be determined, they will have the same opportunities of any child of any heritage. You can see that through the NHL. Jarome Iginla is one of the best players in the league right now. He's one of the few African Canadian players in the league."

What would he be doing if sports wasn't apart of his life? *"I'm a very determined person and a very hard working person. I have no idea what I'd be doing but I would like to be doing something that would be making a difference. I like positions of high pressure. I like being in control. I'd rather own a small company, make a small salary, and be in charge of everything than be at the bottom of the food chain of a big company and have everyone tell me what to do. I feel you make more of a difference when you're in control. That's basically what I'm going to look into doing after hockey - to have something that I choose to do will be my own and I'll be able to run it."*

Damon Stoudamire

National Basketball Association Guard
Damon Stoudamire Foundation www.stoudamire.com

Damon Stoudamire is a media arts major and advocate of the
American Red Cross and Stay in School programs. His foundation
benefits youth in both Ontario and Portland.

When the State of Oregon slashed its budgets in 2002, schools
faced the possibility of cutbacks to extracurricular activities.
Because it's where Stoudamire got his start as a basketball player,
he stepped in and donated $250,000 to the Portland Public
School district.

Purchasing toys and clothing for young students in the Albina Head
Start Classroom, playing Santa and singing songs - these are
activities Stoudamire enjoys to do with kids. He adopts close to 50
children to take on a shopping spree for toys each year - giving
them a $300 gift card for Toys R Us. He's actively involved in
team functions, such as the Blazers Holiday Express, where nearly
200 families were served Thanksgiving dinner.

Through a community-based organization, Stoudamire hosts a
drive to provide school supplies to impoverished children and
teachers Portland at-risk schools. The Damon Stoudamire Celebrity
Bowl-A-Thon raises money for the same association - Schoolhouse
Supplies. He also hosts the Damon Stoudamire Red Cross Blood
Drive on Martin Luther King Jr. Day and encourages African
Americans to donate blood.

Stoudamire sponsors an art exhibit of African American art and
artists for Black History Month plus several basketball camps in
Portland neighborhoods.

Kurt Thomas

National Basketball Association Forward/Center
The Kurt Thomas Foundation

In partnership with Merrill Lynch, The Kurt Thomas Investment Challenge gives New York City high school students the opportunity to participate in the Stock Market Game - the largest stock market simulation program in the United States. About 500,000 students from grades four through 12 participate nationwide. Summer internships are offered to some of the participating students and Thomas rang the trading bell at the New York Stock Exchange for the 2003 kickoff.

Thomas gives four seats and an autographed ball to an underprivileged family in the Have a Ball with Kurt Thomas program. He is an active member of the NBA Read to Achieve program.

Antoine Walker

National Basketball Association Forward
The 8 Foundation

Joanne McClendon and her four children were horrified to discover their Chicago home had been burglarized just a week before Christmas. All the presents from under the tree were stolen. Antoine Walker realized how difficult it would be for this mother to replace them so he personally replenished the gifts in time for the holiday.

Walker was raised with six siblings by a single mother and understands first-hand the challenges faced by inner-city communities. It's why he formed The 8 Foundation - to foster positive life experiences to inner-city youth and support to single parents. Free week-long basketball camps, funding to cash-strapped AAU basketball teams, and the Dorothy Walker Scholarship (in honor of his late grandmother) are just a few of the ways Walker gives back to the Boston and Chicago communities.

The Real Deal Program rewards over 1,000 at-risk Boston Public middle school students who volunteer in neighborhood community service programs. Walker believes this giving back to the community teaches valuable lessons of teamwork and goal setting.

Walker was grateful to receive the NBA's Community Assist Award in June 2002. *"Being recognized for my efforts in the community is very uplifting. I started The 8 Foundation with the hopes of making a real difference, and I take this responsibility very seriously. I would like to thank the NBA, the Celtics, and the staff of The 8 Foundation for their support."*

Chris Webber

National Basketball Association Forward
The Chris Webber Foundation

Chris Webber may have a psychology major from Michigan, his own record label (Humility Records), and even his own comic book (Webber's World), but he knows what it's like to be poor.

He has donated over 300 pairs of children's shoes and supplied gifts and meals for 1,500 people at a Christmas dinner for families in need. He provides tickets for underprivileged youth to attend Sacramento Kings games in the C-Webb's Crew section. Over 2,000 youth and their families have attended games thanks to Webber.

A 16-year-old boy from Guam, through the Make-A-Wish Foundation, asked to see a Kings game, but he got more than he bargained for. Webber brought the boy and his family to the rink the day before and shot hoops with him before fitting him with a Kings jersey and pair of shoes.

Webber's Workshop is an educational event that allows youth to share in the diversity and leadership through hands-on activities.

Youth are broken into small groups overseen by celebrity speakers or educators.

The Chris Webber Foundation was founded to assist troubled youth in Detroit, Michigan, Webber's hometown. It offers scholarships to students striving to do their best both in the classroom and in the community.

Webber bought a collection of African-American documents and artifacts that he shares with others. He puts them on display for fans and underprivileged groups to enjoy. America's oldest art museum west of the Mississippi, Sacramento's Crocker Art Museum, offered to exhibit the collection in early 2003. Over 7,000 had viewed the pieces after just one week.

The Kings/Oscar Robertson Triple-Double Award is presented to a Kings player exemplifying team leadership, all-around game and the spirit of sportsmanship (Triple - On the Court) plus a commitment to community service and family (Double - Off the Court). Webber was the 2003 recipient and he was also awarded the NBA Community Assist in February 2003.

Corliss Williamson

National Basketball Association Forward
Legends of the Rock

Legends of The Rock is a fundraiser established in 2002, where Corliss Williamson and fellow Arkansas alumni help raise funds for youth-oriented programs. It includes planned summer events and working with kids to develop basketball techniques, basic life skills, teamwork, and empowerment tools.

Williamson's generosity extends well beyond mentoring at-risk youth in his summer camps. He directly contributes significant dollars back to the community on many occasions.

For instance in the 2002-03 season alone:

- $1 million was presented to the Boys and Girls Club of Arkansas River Valley to help build a $3 million dollar facility for youth. Williamson challenged the community to match his gift to help make the facility a reality.
- $10,000 to Keith Jackson's P.A.R.K. Program (Positive Attitude Reaches Kids)
- $10,000 to Tidwell Project (a local dance group of at-risk children)
- $5,000 to Martin Luther King, Jr. Commission
- $2,500 to Sweet Dreams Project
- $1,500 to the Hope Christian Community Foundation
- $1,500 to AAU Rockets (girls basketball team)
- $1,500 to AAU LR Bulls (boys basketball team)

A co-captain of the Detroit Pistons All-Star Read to Achieve Reading Team, Williamson represented the club with the Detroit PAL (Police Athletic League). He spent two hours reading and working on computers with the kids during the unveiling of the PAL's Pistons sponsored Reading and Learning Center.

Williamson was on hand when 300 metro-Detroit fourth and fifth grade students participated in a reading party and holiday screening of *Harry Potter and the Chamber of Secrets*. He is also actively involved with numerous public service announcements.

Stephane Yelle

National Hockey Association Center

Stephane Yelle is quiet and unassuming but his character speaks volumes both on and off the ice. He hosts his own golf tournament in Ottawa each summer and supports other charity tournaments.

"I grew up in a small French town east of Ottawa with a population of maybe, 1,500 people. My parent's were teachers. My uncles were

involved in teaching so school was a big factor when I was growing up. My older brother and my two sisters - they all went to college. I was playing hockey, but at the same time, I saw college or university as my future. But when I got the chance to play hockey, eventually I had to quit college to get into professional hockey.

"Who I looked up to...mostly it was my parents and my family. I was really focused on school, which kept me straight. They involved me in hockey starting at four or five years old. Hockey was my pastime. We lived across a schoolyard where there was an outdoor rink. When I finished my homework, I'd spend three or four hours on the ice. That's how I passed my time.

"I followed Wayne Gretzky for a long time. The Oilers were my favorite team. When I made it (to the NHL) and got to play against him...I remember the first time I took a face-off against him. It was weird to have an idol and then finally get to play against him.

"Being involved in charities means a lot to me, to be able to give back to everybody in the community, but mostly to kids. Back home, I have a golf tournament that we've done for five or six years. The money goes to the school to buy books, if they need new playground apparel - whatever the needs are for kids around the community. I'm involved with other charities. There were some in Denver when I played for the Avalanche. It makes me feel good to be able to give back to some needy kids. They're the ones that are suffering. They're the ones that have the challenges.

"There are numerous stories. The best times I've had was when I was involved with kids and the Avalanche when we did the Children's Hospital visits just before

Stephane
Yelle

Christmas every year. It was just overwhelming to see the parents, the kids, and what they go through. It makes me realize how lucky we are to be able to do what we're doing. It's a game, it's our job, but we're lucky to be able to do this. It's just awesome to go to the hospital to see those kids, their smiles. A lot of times, the kids are really sick. Maybe they don't appreciate it as much as they could because they're really sick. It means a lot to the parents. You see them smiling for a little bit.

"I was doing charity stuff in my first few years and I got to play with Shjon Podein. He's really involved with charities and he's got one for a disease called, Ataxia (a muscular disease the Podein Foundation supports). It's a big fundraiser back in Rochester, Minnesota, where he's from. It's the Shjon Podein Children's Foundation. Just from seeing how involved he was and how passionate he was, I went along with him and try to participate in the stuff he does.

"My parents always brought us up to give back. Anyway you can give back is really positive."

Conclusion

During a broadcast of an NCAA football game, the commentators talked about Todd Williams, the Florida State University offensive lineman who was working on two degrees - in sociology and criminology. His story was a testament to how sports can change lives.

His grandmother, who died when he was only 15 years old, raised Williams, who was abandoned by his mother. Homeless and desperate, he was about to steal money out of a house when he stopped to see Florida State playing a game on a television. That moment became the turning point in his life. Rather than succumbing to a life of crime, he decided to ask for help.

Williams went to high school and in his senior year, turned heads as one of Florida's top offensive line prospects. The Florida Times-Union listed him as the fifth top offensive tackle in the state. An FSU coach spotted him and Williams was offered a football scholarship.

While his freshman year (1999) produced sporadic playing time, Williams saw action in all 12 games in his sophomore season before suiting up for his team's appearance in the Orange Bowl. In his junior year (2001), he registered 30 pancake blocks and 10 key blocks and started every game at tackle before he was moved to a split tackle position.

Peyton Manning owns every passing record at University of Tennessee. Following his father's footsteps (Archie Manning who spanned a 14-year NFL career as one of the league's best quarterbacks), it was a matter of time before the NFL would be knocking on his door. When they did, Manning chose to keep them at bay. He opted to finish his senior year of college in lieu of signing a multi-million dollar contract with the New York Jets. Scouts and agents were appalled at the thought of this talented prospect throwing away millions of dollars. Manning eventually signed an NFL contract and shunned his critics by putting up incredible numbers - enough to put him in the NFL record book in only his first few seasons.

Emmitt Smith was in the middle of his football career when he graduated from the University of Florida with a degree in public recreation. Vince Carter created a stir when he chose to attend his graduation ceremony at University of North Carolina - the morning of Game Seven of the Eastern Conference semi-finals when the Toronto Raptors faced the Philadelphia 76ers. Carter still made the game and scored 20 points although the Raptors lost when he missed a game winning shot as the buzzer sounded.

For those who criticize society's obsession with celebrity culture, these four individuals are very strong examples of how athletes can become role models. On the average, a professional career may last two to three years. These players all chose to place a strong importance on education so they would have something to fall back on later.

Being in the public eye means that everything that athlete does is magnified ten times that of an average person. Whether they like it or not, kids look up to them. Even adults. On numerous occasions, I have listened to someone trash professional players, calling them money-hungry jerks, and then when a professional athlete walks into his presence, his demeanor immediately changes. You can see his eyes light up and he immediately becomes a fan.

One of the stories that captured my attention is that of NHL goalie, Jamie Storr. He hones the point that, until people see themselves in their role models, it's hard to imagine the possibility that they could achieve the same goals. In other words, if you never see an African-American basketball player in the NBA, how can an African-American child believe his dream of playing professionally is a realistic one? Japanese-Canadians know it's possible they can play in the NHL because they can see Jamie and Paul Kariya. Slovakian kids can dream of playing in the NBA because they see Vlade Divac. Thanks for reading and may all your hopes and dreams come true.

Debbie Elicksen

Bibliography

Adelson, Joseph (Edited by). Handbook of Adolescent Psychology. John Wiley & Sons, New York, 1980

Associated Press, Los Angeles. Kobe's millions could dry up fast. Calgary Herald, July 20, 2003

Associated Press, New York. Sports leaders want to aim high for young fans. Calgary Herald, January 31, 1997

Associated Press, Los Angeles. Shaq slap sparks suspension. Laker star to miss one game, fined $10,000. Calgary Herald, November 4, 1997

Bandura, Albert. Perceived Self-Efficacy in the Exercise of Personal Agency. Journal of Applied Sports Psychology, Vol. 2, Issue 2, Pages 117-148

Bandura, Albert. The Psychology of Chance Encounters and Life Paths. American Psychologist, July 1982, Vol. 37, No. 7, Pages 747-755

Bandura, Albert; Ross, Dorothea; Ross, Sheila A. Imitation of Film-Mediated Aggressive Models. Journal of Abnormal and Social Psychology, Vol. 66, Pages 3-11, 1963

Benson, Peter L. All Kids are Our Kids. What communities must do to raise caring and responsible children and adolescents. Jossey-Bass Publishers, San Francisco, 1997

Binder, Sarah. Name brands rule among savvy students. Canadian Press, Montreal, November 4, 1997

Bragg, Robert. Teenagers don't deserve to be stereotyped. Calgary Herald, November 27, 1997

Braun, Jerry. School sports build better students. Calgary Herald, February 24, 1977

Bussey, Kay; Bandura, Albert. Influence of Gender Constancy and Social Power on Sex-Linked Modeling. Journal of Personality and Social Psychology, Vol. 47, Pages 1292-1302, 1984

Cameron, Allen. Money changes everything. Cost may drive Okotoks slider from circuit. Calgary Herald, February 16, 2001

Campbell, Janet (Retired teacher and elementary school principal). Promote only successful students. No-fail policy ensures rise in illiteracy rates and loss of self-esteem. Guest column, Calgary Herald, August 6, 1996

Center for Sports Parenting. www.sportsparenting.org

Chicago Tribune. www.chicagotribune.com

Christie, James. "Sit down and shut up," Chretien tells minister. Globe and Mail.com, posted February 20, 2003

Christie, James. Athletes tell Ottawa to take a high jump. Globe and Mail.com, posted February 21, 2003

Cryderman, Kelly. Sociologist's Report: Jock wives face "culture of adultery". Calgary Herald, August 21, 2001

Dawson, Chris. Many teens highly stressed (Psychiatric Study). Calgary Herald, October 7, 1993

Deacon, James. Spoiled Sports. Maclean's Cover, Macleans.ca, February 17, 2003

Doup, Liz. Cheaters do prosper. South Florida Sun-Sentinel, Fort Lauderdale, Florida, published in Calgary Herald, June 23, 2003

Dowbiggin, Bruce. Adults on both sides should learn lesson. Calgary Herald, April 11, 2002

Dowbiggin, Bruce. Kids need to know the score. Calgary Herald, November 11, 2002

Ewing, Lori. Life just got a little easier. Sponsorship money just what amateurs need to pay bills. Calgary Herald, January 31, 1997

Feschuk, Dave. Artwork in the NBA. National Post, November 30, 2002

Florida State Seminoles. Todd Williams profile, http://seminoles.ocsn.com/sports/m-footbl/mtt/williams_todd00.html

Frank, Charles. Whatever happened to letting kids have some fun? Calgary Herald, May 3, 1997

Friscolanti, Michael. Little League protests police checks. National Post, October 10, 2002

Goldstein, Arnold P. Delinquent Gangs. Psychological Perspective. Research Press, Champaign, Illinois, 1991

Gram, Karen. Ruled by their peers. Calgary Herald, Southam Newspapers, Vancouver, July 2, 1997

Herald News Services. Payton guilty of assault. Calgary Herald, June 4, 2003

Hickey, Pat. Controversy follows father figures. Women's stars often have to fight to escape shadow of overbearing dads. Montreal Gazette, August 19, 2002

Konotopetz, Gyle. Winning at any cost wrong message: Renny. Coach wants kids to have a more enjoyable environment. Calgary Herald, December 6, 1998

Maki, Al. Cutting out sports a game plan for disaster.
Calgary Herald, January 30, 1997

Marcia, James E. Development and Validation of Ego Identity
Status. Journal of Personality and Social Psychology, Vol. 3,
Pages 551-558, 1966

Marshall, Andy. School sports at risk. Calgary Herald,
January 28, 1997

Mitchell, John J. The Nature of Adolescence. Detselig Enterprises
Limited, Calgary, Alberta, 1986

Mosham, David (Educational Psychology, University of Nebraska).
Identity as a Theory of Oneself. The Genetic Epistemologist,
Journal of the Jean Piaget Society, Vol. 26, No. 3, 1998

National Football League. Peyton Manning bio, www.nfl.com,
http://www.nfl.com/players/playerpage/12531/bios

National Football League. Emmitt Smith bio, www.nfl.com, http://
www.nfl.com/players/playerpage/1094/bios

Osman, Karen. Gangs. Lucent Books, San Diego, 1992

Padilla, Felix M. The Gang as an American Enterprise.
Rutgers University Press, New Brunswick, New Jersey, 1992

Parcels, Jim (An analysis of "What Hockey Doesn't Have to
Offer"). Straight facts about making it in pro hockey.
CBC: The Fifth Estate, January 1999

Pollack, William, Ph. D. Real Boys. Rescuing Our Sons from the
Myths of Boyhood. An Owl Book, Henry Holt and Company,
New York, 1998

Pollack, William, Ph. D; Cushman, Kathleen. Real Boys Workbook. The Definitive Guide to Understanding and Interacting with Boys of All Ages. Villard Books, New York, 2001

Polzer, Tim and Seeholzer, Don. Dennis Green: Better coaching through chemistry. NFL Insider, NFLHS.com, August 2, 2002

Rauw, Murray. Winning at all costs a fine line to walk. Coaches can cross over to bully role. Calgary Herald, October 17, 2002

Robertson-Wilson, Jennifer; Cote, Jean—for the Canadian Hockey Association (Canadian University Partnership Program/Canadian Hockey Research Program). The Role of Parents in Children's Hockey Participation. Queen's University, Kingston, Ontario, June 2002

Roberts, Siobhan. How athletes' wives handle culture of adultery. Response to cheating depends on reasons for marriage. National Post, August 21, 2001

Smyth, Julie. Busy pupils go farther, studies show. National Post, September 2001

Statistics Canada. www.statcan.ca. Canadian statistics – Justice and crime—victims, suspects, and criminals: Charges by type of offence: Persons charged by type of offence: Rate of youths charged and Rate of adults charged

Summerfield, Robin. Sport study targets motivation factor. Calgary Herald, October 20, 2002

Todd, Douglas. Sports, being quasi-religious, can promote good or bad. Calgary Herald, August 1, 1999

Zickefoose, Sherri. Vince has 'bean' there… Calgary Herald, July 17, 2003

Interviews

Bylsma, Dan, National Hockey League player
Clay, April, Chartered Psychologist
Egener, Mike, Western Hockey League player
Gilmour, Doug, National Hockey League player
Iginla, Jarome, National Hockey League player
Juneau, Joe, National Hockey League player
Kariya, Paul, National Hockey League player
Krause, Jayson, Canadian National Bobsleigh Team
Laperriere, Ian, National Hockey League player
McLoughlin, Mark, Canadian Football League player
McNabb, Corey, Hockey Canada Initiation Program
O'Ree, Willie, National Hockey League Diversity Task Force
Sawatzky, Garry, Canadian Football League player
Storr, Jamie, National Hockey League player
Wong, Helen, National Baskeball Association, Senior Manager
International PR
Yelle, Stephane, National Hockey League player

Websites

www.adonalfoyle.com
www.allanhouston.com
www.antawnjamison.net
www.bobteamkrause.ca
www.briangrant44.com
www.cfl.ca
www.danbylsma.com
www.future-foundation.com
www.givingback.org
www.gpfoundation.org
www.hitmenhockey.com
www.hockeycanada.ca

www.hockeyitpays.com
www.jalenrosefoundation.org
www.jerrystackhouse.com
www.juwanhoward.com
www.larryhughesfoundation.com
www.mlb.com
www.nba.com
www.nhl.com
www.sixers.com
www.stoudamire.com
www.t-mac.com
www.vincecarter15.com

About the author

A publisher, author, and writer, Debbie Elicksen covers the Calgary Flames and the National Hockey League regularly as a reporter, which includes filing reports for The Fischler Report, and Sportsticker.

She has spent several years working in both amateur and professional sports administration in hockey, baseball, and football. Playing a key role in junior football in Canada (17-22 year olds, post-secondary) for over 16 years, she was the first woman to headman a football conference in Canada - the Prairie Football Conference. As President and Assistant General Manager of the Calgary Colts, she became known as a strong administrator, lobbying for on-field and off-field improvements throughout the league. Her duties included on-field and off-field activities, overseeing game day operations, business and football operations, public relations, managing equipment, team travel arrangements, negotiating coaching salaries, and even negotiating a team into the conference (Winnipeg Hawkeyes).

As Public Relations Director for the Edmonton Trappers Baseball Club, she worked closely with the California Angels and was responsible for overseeing game day operations, media liaison, and community events. She was a volunteer media liaison for the hockey committee during 1988 Winter Olympic Games in Calgary. As a mentor with the Alberta Mentor Foundation for Youth, she meets one-on-one with a junior high or high school student each week. She was recognized as Volunteer Mentor of the Year for 2001-2002 and received the inaugural Garry and Kathy Sawatzky Mentor Award in 2003.

Reader survey

This book came about after witnessing first-hand the positive effects of sport in general. In my exposure to National Hockey League players, I've watched many of them give back to the community as much as they can. One example is Jarome Iginla. Long after his teammates and the media are gone from the locker room, Jarome is signing autographs on numerous articles the Public Relations department uses for giveaways. He donates $1,000 to Kidsport Calgary for each goal he scores, donates his time to play wheelchair basketball with the kids at the Children's Hospital, runs his own hockey school as part of the NHL Diversity program, participates in numerous golf tournaments, including one for Juvenile Diabetes, and tries to sign as many autographs as he can, even while others are impatiently waiting for him.

While not every professional athlete is a pillar of the community, a good majority remember what it was like when they looked up to their heroes. For others outside of the professional sports realm, sport offers a sense of belonging, teaches discipline, and how to get along with others, but most of all, it gives kids the skills they need to take into the real world - to become better citizens and perhaps, future role models.

I would like to know what you think about this book by completing the following reader survey. I appreciate your taking the time to do this and especially for taking the time to read this book.

Debbie Elicksen

Send Reader Survey to:

> Debbie Elicksen
> Freelance Communications
> #45, 3809 – 45 Street SW, Calgary, Alberta, T3E 3H4 Canada
> Fax: (403) 249-4249
> Email: delicksen@shaw.ca   www.freelancepublishing.net

Reader Survey

On a scale of 5, the degree to which this book met my expectations is: (circle one of the numbers)

Met expectations 5 4 3 2 1   Did not meet expectations

Favorite story in the book

_____

Most inspiring story

_____

Biggest misconception about professional athletes before reading the book

_____

Best idea/lesson learned from the book

_____

Overall comments and feedback

_____

Suggestions for future sports books

_____

Favorite professional team

_____

Favorite professional athlete

_____

Favorite personality

_____

What they're saying about *Inside the NHL Dream*

"I really like this book and one of the reasons why is, she touches on all aspects of the pro game. She talks about a lot of the great players in the game-coaches, management, all these people and talks about all the different elements. I thought it was really cool."

Kelly Hrudey

"You told it like it is. The NHL is full of great athletes that have paid the price, appreciate it and give it back. Everyone we see, players we meet, I am very grateful that I have been given the chance to allow my son to meet young men from other countries by way of the NHL and by reading books like yours, showing him that, no matter what you want to do in the future, it takes hard work. "

M. Bonema

"A must read - tells it like it is. Thorough, thoughtful, insightful. More than a peek - a long penetrating stare at contemporary hockey's grass roots and underpinnings...superbly presented."

Art Breeze, Pro-REP Entertainment Group

"When I picked your book up on Saturday morning I had absolutely no intention of reading it cover to cover in one sitting. The telephone was ringing and e-mails were piling up as is usual in my life. Still, I was so entranced with the player commentary that I could not put the book down. Next time I am at a hockey game I will most certainly view every aspect of the game in a different light because of your book."

CSM

Biggest misconception before reading the book:
"Overpaid, spoiled athletes"
Best idea/lesson learned from book:
"How players adjust to fans' huge expectations"
Overall comments: "Well researched & great presentation"

M. Thorpe

"I want to thank you for taking the time for writing a book that is long overdue. Thank you from all hockey fans."

B. J. McKee

"As a player-agent, I particularly enjoyed Chapter 4—The Agent's Role, and I enjoyed your style of writing."

Bobby Orr

THE CALGARY BOOSTER CLUB:
Creating a legacy for
local sports (ISBN 0-9730237-2-4)

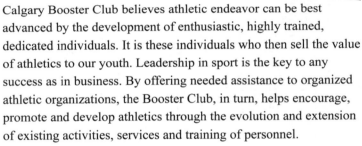

**Available through McNally
Robinson bookstore, Calgary
www.calgaryboosterclub.com**

Athletics play a critical role in developing
the character of our youth. It also adds to
the cohesiveness of our community. The
Calgary Booster Club believes athletic endeavor can be best
advanced by the development of enthusiastic, highly trained,
dedicated individuals. It is these individuals who then sell the value
of athletics to our youth. Leadership in sport is the key to any
success as in business. By offering needed assistance to organized
athletic organizations, the Booster Club, in turn, helps encourage,
promote and develop athletics through the evolution and extension
of existing activities, services and training of personnel.

This book will generate awareness and excitement about Calgary's
rich sport history and create a legacy for future generations.
Readers will have a first-hand account of the growth of Calgary's
amateur athletic programs and a greater appreciation for the
achievement of athletes and the efforts of volunteers, coaches,
officials, administrators, and builders of sport.

This book is part of a celebration of all that has been accomplished
by the Booster Club over the past 50 years…the enthusiasm of the
early years, the encouragement of emerging sport groups, the
excitement and heady years of the Olympic bids and the
organization of the Games.

FREELANCE COMMUNICATIONS
Self-Publishing Services

There are many tools to uniqueness and creativity - one is through the use of books. Books offer perceived credibility and expertise in your field. However, book publishing takes a great deal of time and money. It is not for the faint of heart. There are four types of publishing:

- Royalty (traditional publishing houses) -author is paid a royalty but the *publisher has creative control* with respect to content, design, marketing and distribution
- Vanity -publish anyone who pays for printing and binding with *no editing, marketing, or distribution support*
- Subsidy (joint venture, co-publisher) -author pays for printing and binding but publisher may subsidize some costs, however, *completed books are property of publisher* and author receives royalty when sold
- Selp-publishing -while author undertakes cost of publication and handles all marketing, distribution and warehousing, *the author has exclusive creative control and receives 100 percent of sale proceeds* (Note: Booksellers usually take 45 percent of cover price while distributor takes 10 percent)

Freelance Communication provides full publishing support to self-publishers who want to get their message across in books. We've already done the legwork in getting the best quotes for quality work.

Debbie Elicksen
#45, 3809 - 45 St. SW
Calgary, Alberta
T3E 3H4

Phone: 403- 240-1340
Fax: 403-249-4249
Cell: 403-807-1984
delicksen@shaw.ca
freelancepublishing.net

Authors can choose from the following services:

- Full project management
- Graphic design and layout
- ISBN and National Library Cataloguing
- Writing and editing
- Marketing and distribution planning and support
- Printing

Freelance Communications collaborated with Brian Lee on "K.E.E.P. Your Nurses For Life", published September 2001. The following books are on its publishing list:

- Inside the NHL Dream - ISBN 0-9730237-0-8 (released September 2002)
- The Calgary Booster Club. Creating a legacy for local sport - ISBN 0-9730237-2-4 (released March 2003)
- Positive Sports: Professional athletes and mentoring youth - ISBN 0-9730237-3-2 (October 2003)